Colossians:
navigating successfully through cultural chaos

Bible Study That Builds Christian Community

ISBN: 1-5749-4136-4

DEWEY: 227.7
SUBHD: BIBLE. N.T. COLOSSIANS--STUDY \ CHRISTIAN LIFE

Unless otherwise indicated, Scripture quotations are taken from
the *Holman Christian Standard Bible*, © copyright 2000 by
Holman Bible Publishers. Used by permission.

To order additional copies of this resource:
ORDER ONLINE at *www.serendipityhouse.com*;
VISIT the LifeWay Christian Store serving you;
WRITE Serendipity House
117 10th Avenue, North
Nashville, TN 37234
FAX (615) 277-8181
PHONE (800) 525-9563

Printed in the United States of America

117 10th Avenue, North
Nashville, Tennessee 37234

Contents

Core Values

Community: The purpose of this curriculum is to build community within the body of believers around Jesus Christ.

Group Process: To build community, the curriculum must be designed to take a group through a step-by-step process of sharing your story with one another.

Interactive Bible Study: To share your "story," the approach to Scripture in the curriculum needs to be open-ended and right-brained—to "level the playing field" and encourage everyone to share.

Developmental Stages: To provide a healthy program in the life cycle of a group, the curriculum needs to offer courses on three levels of commitment:

(1) **Beginner Level**—low-level entry, high structure, to level the playing field;

(2) **Growth Level**—deeper Bible study, flexible structure, to encourage group accountability;

(3) **Discipleship Level**—in-depth Bible study, open structure, to move the group into high gear.

Target Audiences: To build community throughout the culture of the church, the curriculum needs to be flexible, adaptable, and transferable into the structure of the average church.

Mission: To expand the kingdom of God one person at a time by filling the "empty chair." (We add an extra chair to each group session to remind us of our mission.)

Group Covenant

It is important that your group covenant together, agreeing to live out important group values. Once these values are agreed upon, your group will be on its way to experiencing Christian community. It's very important that your group discuss these values—preferably as you begin this study. The first session would be most appropriate. (Check the rules to which each member of your group agrees.)

- [ ] **Priority:** While you are in this course of study, you give the group meetings priority.
- [ ] **Participation:** Everyone is encouraged to participate and no one dominates.
- [ ] **Respect:** Everyone is given the right to his or her own opinion, and all questions are encouraged and respected.
- [ ] **Confidentiality:** Anything that is said in the meeting is never repeated outside the meeting.
- [ ] **Life Change:** We will regularly assess our own life-change goals and encourage one another in our pursuit of Christlikeness.
- [ ] **Empty Chair:** The group stays open to reaching new people at every meeting.
- [ ] **Care and Support:** Permission is given to call upon each other at any time, especially in times of crisis. The group will provide care for every member.
- [ ] **Accountability:** We agree to let the members of the group hold us accountable to the commitments we make in whatever loving ways we decide upon.
- [ ] **Mission:** We will do everything in our power to start a new group.
- [ ] **Ministry:** The group will encourage one another to volunteer and serve in a ministry and to support missions by giving financially and/or personally serving.

notes

Outrageous Anticipation

Prepare for the Session

	READINGS	REFLECTIVE QUESTIONS
Monday	Colossians 1:1-8	What is happening in your faith or in the faith of a loved one that makes you thankful today?
Tuesday	Psalm 42:1-5	What has been bringing you down recently? How does your faith lift you back up?
Wednesday	Isaiah 40:28-31	In what way do you need God to "renew your strength" for the weeks ahead?
Thursday	Romans 5:3-5	What have you hoped in that has disappointed you? How is your hope in Christ different?
Friday	Romans 8:18-25	What signs of hope do you see in the world around you?
Saturday	1 Peter 1:3-5	To what degree is your hope built on what God has done in Jesus Christ?
Sunday	Revelation 21:1-5	How important is it to you that God will bring about "a new heaven and a new earth"? What encourages you most about this promise?

BIBLE STUDY
- to consider the importance of personal affirmation to Christian fellowship
- to give some thought to the role of hope in relation to love and faith
- to learn about the beginning of the church at Colossae

LIFE CHANGE
- to find three new Christians to affirm in their new faith
- to testify to the hope within us
- to write a letter to ourselves affirming our own growth in the faith

Icebreaker

10-15 minutes

GATHERING
THE PEOPLE
U Form
horseshoe
groups of
6–8 people.

A Good Reputation. Go around the group on question 1 and let everyone share. Then go around again on questions 2 and 3, as time allows.

1. By the time you were in high school, what did you have a reputation for?

☐ high academic achievement ☐ lack of achievement
☐ high athletic achievement ☐ my Christian character
☐ high musical achievement ☐ my sense of humor
☐ my rebelliousness ☐ hard work
☐ my prowess with the opposite sex
☐ the creativity I showed in getting into trouble
☐ other: _____

2. As an adult, in what area of your life have you worked hardest at building your reputation?

☐ in my professional life ☐ in my family life
☐ in my political influence ☐ in my spiritual life
☐ in my community involvement ☐ in my character
☐ other: _____

3. If the people who know you best were asked what you are known for today, what would they say?

Bible Study

30-45 minutes

The Scripture for this week:

LEARNING FROM THE BIBLE

COLOSSIANS 1:1–8

¹Paul, an apostle of Christ Jesus by God's will, and Timothy our brother:

²To the saints and faithful brothers in Christ in Colossae. Grace to you and peace from God our Father.

³We always thank God, the Father of our Lord Jesus Christ, when we pray for you, ⁴for we have heard of your faith in Christ Jesus and of the love you have for all the saints ⁵because of the hope reserved for you in heaven. You have already heard about this hope in the message of truth, ⁶the gospel that has come to you. It is bearing fruit and growing all over the world, just as it has among you since the day you heard it and recognized God's grace in the truth. ⁷You learned this from Epaphras, our much loved fellow slave. He is a faithful minister of the Messiah on your behalf, ⁸and he has told us about your love in the Spirit.

...about today's session

A WORD FROM THE LEADER

Write your answers here.

1. When are people most likely to commit suicide?

2. On what inadequate sources of hope have people sometimes relied?

3. What does true hope require?

Identifying with the Story

In horseshoe groups of 6–8, explore questions as time allows.

1. Who is someone you thank God for when you pray? What characteristic does this person have that you especially appreciate?

2. Who, above everyone else, is most responsible for you hearing and understanding the hope of the gospel of Jesus Christ? What did this person say or do that influenced you?

3. When it comes to thanking others for what they have done or are doing, how do you show your appreciation?

   ☐ send them a thank you note or personal letter
   ☐ pull them aside and tell them face-to-face
   ☐ do something for them to show my thanks
   ☐ do nothing, and just assume they know
   ☐ remind them of what they *have not* done—I don't want them to rest on their laurels!
   ☐ other: _____

today's session

What is God teaching you from this story?

1. Who established the church at Colossae? What seems to have been the nature of Paul's relationship to this church?

2. What did Paul thank God for in this church?

3. What two tools do people use to influence others? Which approach did Paul almost always use first in his letters?

4. In what two ways does our Christian hope intensify the love we have for fellow Christians?

_____

_____

5. Where else in his letters did Paul speak of the importance of Christian hope to faith?

Learning from the Story

⚘ In horseshoe groups of 6-8, choose an answer and explain why you chose what you did.

1. If someone told you that they had heard of "the love your church has for all the saints," what would be your reaction?

☐ They obviously have not been to our board meetings.
☐ The saints, maybe, but we have a hard time loving those sinners.
☐ The love is real—but we need to work on our faith more.
☐ I would not be surprised—the love is what brought me here.

2. In what way has the hope you have heard and learned about in the gospel born fruit (had visible results) in your life?

3. Where do you see the gospel growing and spreading today? In what way do you feel called to help the good news of Christ grow?

life change lessons

How can you apply this session to your life?

Write your answers here.

1. In what two ways have Christian leaders sometimes emphasized the negative over the positive?

_____

_____

2. What is often the result of trying to motivate people by such a negative approach?

Caring Time
15-20 minutes

CARING TIME

⋃ Remain in horseshoe groups of 6-8.

This is the time for developing and expressing your caring for each other. Begin by having group members finish this sentence:

*"The hope I have for what will happen in this class
in the weeks to come is ..."*

Pray for these hopes, as well as the concerns that are listed on the Prayer/Praise Report. Include prayer for the empty chair, and ask God to guide you to someone to invite for next week.

If you would like to pray silently, say "Amen" when you have finished your prayer, so that the next person will know when to start.

BIBLE STUDY NOTES

Reference Notes

Use these notes to gain further understanding
of the text as you study on your own.

COLOSSIANS 1:2

saints. This term is not used in the Roman Catholic sense of those elevated officially to a special status by the church, or in the popular sense of people with morally flawless behavior. Rather the "saints" are all persons sanctified or made holy by the blood of Jesus Christ.

**COLOSSIANS
1:2
(cont'd)**

Colossae. This city lay about 100 miles east of Ephesus in the Lycus River Valley. Since it was located on a major trade route from Ephesus, Colossae was considered a great city in the days of Xerxes, the Persian king (fifth century B.C.). One hundred years later, it had developed into a prosperous commercial center on account of its weaving industry. By the time of Paul, Colossae's prominence had diminished though its sister cities, Laodicea and Hierapolis, were still prospering.

Grace to you and peace. This is a Christianized adaptation of a common greeting. This letter highlights the reality of God's grace through Christ and the reconciliation (peace) that results.

**COLOSSIANS
1:4–5**

faith...love...hope. This triad of Christian graces is arranged and expanded upon in various ways throughout the New Testament (Rom. 5:1-5; 1 Cor. 13:13; Gal. 5:5-6; Eph. 4:2-5; 1 Thess. 1:3,5:8; Heb. 6:10-12; 1 Pet. 1:3-8). The center of the Christian faith is Jesus Christ; the essence of its lifestyle is love; and the sure hope of a future with Christ is its motivation.

**COLOSSIANS
1:6**

bearing fruit. See Mark 4:1-20,26-29.

growing all over the world. Within 30 years after Jesus' resurrection, the gospel had spread from Palestine throughout the Roman Empire.

heard it and recognized God's grace in the truth. The words *all* or *everything* appear repeatedly in 1:1-23. Through this emphasis, Paul is countering the false teachers' claims that there is more to learn and experience about life with God than what can be found in the message of God's grace in Christ (2:4,8).

**COLOSSIANS
1:7**

Epaphras. A native Colossian who established the church there and worked for Christ throughout the Lycus valley (4:12; Philem. 23).

notes

Just Do It

Prepare for the Session

	READINGS	REFLECTIVE QUESTIONS
Monday	Colossians 1:9-10	What do you need to do today to "walk worthy of the Lord"?
Tuesday	Colossians 1:11-12	In what situation will you especially need patience in the coming week?
Wednesday	Colossians 1:13-14	Where do you see a "domain of darkness" in the world around you? In what way(s) have you been part of that darkness?
Thursday	Acts 26:19-20	How has your repentance for past wrongs been reflected in your behavior? What can you do today to demonstrate that repentance is real?
Friday	Galatians 5:22-26	Which fruit of the Spirit are you best manifesting in your life? Which fruit do you need to work on, with the Holy Spirit's help?
Saturday	1 John 3:10b-15	Who are you having difficulty loving right now? What could help you change your attitude toward this person?
Sunday	1 John 5:3-5	Which of God's commandments have you found burdensome? How could obedience to that commandment help you "conquer the world"?

BIBLE STUDY
- to understand that we are called to live in a manner worthy of our Lord Jesus Christ
- to see how living in a manner worthy of Christ requires help and strength from God
- to consider what it means for a Christian life to "bear fruit"

LIFE CHANGE
- to pray daily for the other members of this group and their growth
- to pray for our own spiritual strengthening
- to find one new way to put our faith into action

Icebreaker
10-15 minutes

**GATHERING
THE PEOPLE
ひ Form
horseshoe
groups of
6–8 people.**

Rescue Operation. Go around the group on question 1 and let everyone share. Then go around again on questions 2 and 3, as time allows.

1. When you were in grade school, from what or whom did you most feel the need to be rescued?

   ☐ the demands of my parents ☐ a pesky sibling
   ☐ the opposite sex   ☐ school work
   ☐ the neighborhood bully   ☐ work of any kind
   ☐ my own shyness   ☐ other: _____

2. As an adult, from what or whom do you most feel the need to be rescued?

   ☐ telemarketers and solicitors
   ☐ demanding family members
   ☐ my addiction to sweets and junk food
   ☐ the scary world we live in
   ☐ bills
   ☐ my own bad decisions
   ☐ other: _____

3. If you could be whisked off to a magical kingdom, what would be the most important qualities you would want that kingdom to have?

Bible Study

30-45 minutes

The Scripture for this week:

⁹For this reason also, since the day we heard this, we haven't stopped praying for you. We are asking that you may be filled with the knowledge of His will in all wisdom and spiritual understanding, ¹⁰so that you may walk worthy of the Lord, fully pleasing to Him, bearing fruit in every good work and growing in the knowledge of God. ¹¹May you be strengthened with all power, according to His glorious might, for all endurance and patience, with joy ¹²giving thanks to the Father, who has enabled you to share in the saints' inheritance in the light. ¹³He has rescued us from the domain of darkness and transferred us into the kingdom of the Son He loves, ¹⁴in whom we have redemption, the forgiveness of sins.

...about today's session

A WORD
FROM THE
LEADER

Write your
answers
here.

1. What have Christians down through the ages discovered to be impossible?

2. Why are we to do good works?

3. What characteristics describe the family of God?

Identifying with the Story

In horseshoe groups of 6–8, explore questions as time allows.

1. When you were in grade school, whom did you most want to please by your behavior? Do you remember a time when you did something to disappoint this person? How did you feel, and what did you do?

2. When do you remember receiving an honor that you felt unworthy to receive? What did you do in response?

3. In general, which of the following responses best reflects how worthy you feel of the good things that have happened to you?

   ☐ "What good things?"
   ☐ "What have I ever done to deserve even one of the pleasures I've known?"
   ☐ "Hey, I am as worthy as the next person!"
   ☐ "Basically, I've earned what I've gotten in life."
   ☐ "I deserve much better than I'm getting!"

today's session

What is God teaching you from this story?

1. What are two reasons we should walk in a manner worthy of our Lord?

   _____

   _____

2. What are two qualities of a life of sin that should make us want to avoid that life?

   _____

   _____

3. What are two ways that God helps us to walk worthy of Him?

_____

_____

4. What are the two main elements in walking worthy of the Lord?

_____

_____

5. What is the essence of what it means to walk in a manner worthy of our Lord?

Learning from the Story

⊍ In horseshoe groups of 6-8, choose an answer and explain why you chose what you did.

1. Looking back at your life, when would you say you were most part of a "domain of darkness" (v. 13)? How did Christ rescue you from that time?

2. Where do you feel you are right now in terms of "growing in the knowledge of God" (v. 10)?

☐ I am a tiny sprig of life, freshly emerged from the ground.
☐ I am a little seedling, still tender and vulnerable, but growing fast.
☐ I am a strong, healthy tree, bearing fruit.
☐ I am a diseased tree, alive but struggling to go on.
☐ I am like a giant Sequoia with firm and ancient roots.

3. What do you most need to continue to grow in the Lord?

☐ more knowledge of God and the Bible
☐ more affirmation and encouragement from others in the church
☐ more opportunities to serve God in meaningful ways
☐ more opportunities to explore my questions
☐ more discipline in my prayer and devotional life
☐ other: _____

life change lessons

How can you apply this session to your life?

Write your answers here.

1. What do you acknowledge when you pray for strength and direction?

2. If you were truly to pray as Paul teaches in our Scripture passage for today, how would it change your prayer life?

Caring Time

15-20 minutes

CARING TIME

◊ Remain in horseshoe groups of 6-8.

Begin this prayer time by thanking God for rescuing us from the "domain of darkness" and transferring us into the "kingdom of the Son He loves" (v. 13). Take turns praying for each other, asking God for the strength to "walk worthy of the Lord" and direction to live according to His will. Also, use the Prayer/Praise Report and pray for the concerns listed.

Close by praying specifically for God to guide you to someone to invite for next week to fill the empty chair.

Reference Notes

BIBLE STUDY NOTES

Use these notes to gain further understanding
of the text as you study on your own.

COLOSSIANS 1:9

knowledge/all wisdom and spiritual understanding. The false teachers (combining elements of Christianity, Greek mystery religions, and Judaism) defined salvation in terms of secret, divine knowledge and ecstatic experiences that could only be gained by following their regimen of ascetic disciplines and ceremonies.

COLOSSIANS 1:10

walk worthy of the Lord. Rather than esoteric knowledge and experiences, true spirituality is seen in a lifestyle that reflects the love and holiness of Jesus.

bearing fruit. Scripture is consistent in insisting that the Christian life should bear fruit in works of righteousness. Jesus condemned the fig tree that bore no fruit (Matt. 21:18-22) and praised the soil that bore much produce (Matt. 13:8). Paul detailed the fruit that should be present in a life led by the Spirit: love, joy, peace, patience, kindness, goodness, faithfulness, gentleness, and self-control (Gal. 5:22-23).

COLOSSIANS 1:12

enabled. In the mystery religions, a person supposedly qualified to share in the divine through practicing various rites and disciplines (2:18). By contrast, God fully "enables" the believer to inherit His kingdom through Christ's work.

the saints' inheritance in the light. Other contemporary writings show that this refers to God's angels. Through God's grace, Christians share the heavenly portion enjoyed by the angels, a point denied by the false teachers.

COLOSSIANS 1:13

the domain of darkness. Darkness is an appropriate image for the influence of the hostile spiritual forces (v.16), since their domination only leads to spiritual and moral blindness (Luke 22:53; John 1:5; Eph. 5:8-14).

COLOSSIANS 1:14

redemption. The believers' rescue from the domain of darkness came because Jesus broke its power by His sacrificial death (v. 20; Eph. 1:7).

notes

3

Radical Reconciliation

Prepare for the Session

	READINGS	REFLECTIVE QUESTIONS
Monday	Colossians 1:15-16	What do you see in creation that especially reflects Christ?
Tuesday	Colossians 1:17-18	Is your church allowing Christ to be its true head? When have you usurped Christ's place by trying to control the church yourself?
Wednesday	Colossians 1:19-20	Imagine a completely harmonious and unified creation. How can Christ use you to accomplish this unity?
Thursday	Colossians 1:21-23	What does it mean to you to be "faultless" and "blameless"? Are you letting Christ take away your guilt, or are you holding on to it?
Friday	Romans 8:28-29	In what way, if any, are you more like Christ today than you were five years ago?
Saturday	2 Corinthians 5:17	What aspects of your old, pre-Christ self keep wanting to make a comeback? How does Christ help you claim a victory for a "new you"?
Sunday	Isaiah 11:6-9	What role does knowing God play in harmonious creation? What does this say to you about today's ecological questions?

BIBLE STUDY
- to gain an understanding of Christ's role as the Creator
- to consider God's plan to redeem all of creation
- to see how our own reconciliation to God fits in with God's overall plan of redemption

LIFE CHANGE
- to make sure we are personally right with God
- to act this week to find reconciliation with one other person
- to become involved in a ministry of reconciliation

Icebreaker
10-15 minutes

GATHERING THE PEOPLE
◯ Form horseshoe groups of 6–8 people.

The Center of My Life. Go around the group on question 1 and let everyone share. Then go around again on questions 2 and 3, as time allows.

1. What was the center of your life during the various periods of your life? For each of the categories below, mark "G" if it was the center of your life in grade school, "J" if it was the center of your life in junior high, "H" if it was the center of your life in high school, "YA" if it was the center of your life in your young adult years, and "N" if it is the center of your life now.

____ friends or being popular
____ sports or physical achievements
____ music, drama, or artistic achievements
____ business or professional achievements
____ family
____ money and possessions
____ pets or animals
____ the outdoors/exploring the natural world
____ faith or church gatherings
____ television, movies, or fictional reading
____ other: _____

2. Pick one period of your life and share one way you expressed to others what was at the center of your life (by what you wore, the meetings you went to, what you talked about, etc.)

3. Who shared your passion for the central interest you talked about in the above questions?

Bible Study
30-45 minutes

The Scripture for this week:

¹⁵*He is the image of the invisible God,*
the firstborn over all creation;
¹⁶*because by Him everything was created,*
in heaven and on earth, the visible and the invisible,
whether thrones or dominions or rulers or authorities—
all things have been created through Him and for Him.
¹⁷*He is before all things, and by Him all things hold together.*
¹⁸*He is also the head of the body, the church;*
He is the beginning, the firstborn from the dead,
so that He might come to have first place in everything.
¹⁹*For God was pleased to have all His fullness dwell in Him,*
²⁰*and through Him to reconcile everything to Himself*
by making peace through the blood of His cross —
whether things on earth or things in heaven.
²¹*And you were once alienated and hostile in mind because of your evil actions.* ²²*But now He has reconciled you by His physical body through His death, to present you holy, faultless, and blameless before Him—* ²³*if indeed you remain grounded and steadfast in the faith, and are not shifted away from the hope of the gospel that you heard. This gospel has been proclaimed in all creation under heaven, and I, Paul, have become a minister of it.*

...about today's session

A WORD FROM THE LEADER

Write your answers here.

1. What are some evidences of the disharmony between people and our environment? What are some examples you can think of in addition to those listed?

2. What are some factors that divide us? Are there any others you can think of in addition to those referred to here?

3. What are three aspects of reconciliation in which God wants us to be involved?

_____

_____

_____

Identifying with the Story

♘ **In horseshoe groups of 6–8, explore questions as time allows.**

1. From whom do you feel most alienated at this moment of your life?

☐ a person with whom I work   ☐ my parents
☐ society in general   ☐ a sibling
☐ the government   ☐ my children
☐ my spouse or ex-spouse   ☐ other: _____

2. If you could gauge the sense of harmony you feel with your world right now, where would it be on the following scale?

1 · · · 2 · · · 3 · · · 4 · · · 5 · · · 6 · · · 7 · · · 8 · · · 9 · · · 10

totally in harmony,   totally in discord,
like the best   like a classical pianist
barbershop quartet   in a heavy metal band

26

3. In order to feel more in harmony with the world in which you live, what do you need most?

☐ a whole different world in which to live
☐ a more positive perspective
☐ a willingness to temper my idealism
☐ a vision of where God is taking this world
☐ an ability to love people as they are

today's session ③

What is God teaching you from this story?

1. What word do we use for all of the created order that implies it is a unity?

2. What happened that made people less than what they were created to be—the image of God?

3. How did human sin affect the rest of creation?

4. How did Christ's sacrificial death bring reconciliation to a world in disharmony?

5. What do we need to do before helping our world toward reconciliation?

Learning from the Story

In horseshoe groups of 6-8, choose an answer and explain why you chose what you did.

1. At what point in your life have you felt most alienated from God? How did this feeling of alienation affect your behavior?

2. How quick are you to feel blamed for certain bad things happening?

   ☐ Very quick—the evils of Nazi Germany were probably somehow my fault.

   ☐ Moderately quick—if in doubt, it was my fault.

   ☐ Moderately slow—I can be convinced by the evidence.

   ☐ Very slow—I thought I was wrong once, but I was mistaken!

3. What does it mean to you to be holy? How can you "remain grounded and steadfast in the faith" (v. 23)?

life change lessons

How can you apply this session to your life?

Write your answers here.

1. If someone asked you, "Why can't we all just get along?" what would you answer?

2. What three things can a Christian do to find reconciliation with another person?

   _____

   _____

   _____

Caring Time

15-20 minutes

CARING TIME

U Remain in horseshoe groups of 6-8.

Remember that this is the time for expressing your concern for each other as group members and for supporting one another in prayer. Begin by having each group member answer this question:

"With whom do you need to find reconciliation in the coming week? How can the group pray for you?"

Pray for these needs, as well as the concerns listed on the Prayer/ Praise Report. Remember to pray for God's guidance in inviting someone to the group next week to fill the empty chair.

3

BIBLE STUDY NOTES

Reference Notes

Use these notes to gain further understanding
of the text as you study on your own.

COLOSSIANS 1:15

image of the invisible God. "Image" does not mean a second-hand representation (such as a photograph is an image of a person), but a complete representation: All that God is, Jesus is (John 1:18, 14:9; 2 Cor. 4:4-6; Heb. 1:3). To know God fully, you need not look anywhere else but to Christ.
firstborn. This term had nothing to do with Jesus being created, but meant that Jesus was like the first pioneer into the kingdom that will one day include all who come to God through Jesus.

COLOSSIANS 1:16

thrones or dominions or rulers or authorities. Christ is Lord over all authorities.

COLOSSIANS 1:17

He is before all things. Christ's preeminence means He is Lord over all.
by Him all things hold together. Both Greek and Jewish philosophers were concerned with the "first principles" that gave order and meaning to life. Paul asserts that this is found in Christ (John 1:9).

COLOSSIANS 1:18

the head of the body. This emphasizes the organic, living relationship between Christ and His people.
firstborn. As Jesus is Lord over the original creation, so also he is Lord over the new creation (v. 15).

COLOSSIANS 1:19

fullness. All that can be experienced of God is found in Christ.

reconcile everything to Himself. Jesus seeks the eventual goal of not only reconciling humanity to Himself, but to creation, which has been thrown out of kilter by sin (Rom. 8:19-25).

the blood of His cross. The irony of the gospel is that this cosmic work of redemption was completed through the gory, earthly act of crucifixion.

alienated. Jews viewed Gentile idolatry and immorality as the chief evidence that humanity was in revolt against God. Paul utilized that idea to contrast the Colossians' "before" and "after" status in Christ.

hostile in mind. "Mind" (like the Old Testament word for "heart") represents the core of the personality.

His physical body. The stress is on Jesus' actual body that died, as opposed to the church as the expression of Christ's glorified body (1:18).

holy, faultless, and blameless before Him. While the false teachers taught that the Colossians needed something more in order to be truly spiritual, Paul used the language both of sacrifice and the law court to emphasize that believers are completely acceptable to God through Christ (Rom. 8:1-11).

remain grounded and steadfast in the faith. The work of Christ must be received with faith demonstrated by an ongoing loyalty and obedience to Christ.

proclaimed in all creation under heaven. In face of what the false teachers had said, Paul reassured his readers that they had already received the full gospel as proclaimed everywhere else.

notes

notes

Socially Unacceptable,
Divinely Revered

⊸⊶⊷

Prepare for the Session

	READINGS	REFLECTIVE QUESTIONS
Monday	Colossians 1:24-29	How are you living your life so that others can see Christ in you?
Tuesday	Colossians 2:1-5	Who especially needs your encouragement today? What can you do to give that encouragement?
Wednesday	Luke 10:16	Why does having Christ in you sometimes result in rejection by others? How will you handle such rejection when it occurs?
Thursday	Mark 9:38-41	How have others supported and encouraged you as you have sought to live the Christian life?
Friday	John 14:19-21	How does knowing and remembering that Christ is in you help you to show greater obedience to Him?
Saturday	John 15:18-21	In what ways do you feel persecuted because you are a Christian? How does it help to know that Christ experienced the same things Himself?
Sunday	1 Peter 4:12-13	Have you come to the point where you can say you are glad to suffer for Christ's sake? Why or why not?

BIBLE STUDY

- to discover how Paul responded to the Greek mystery religions that were popular in Colossae
- to consider the role of suffering in furthering the gospel of Christ
- to learn what it means to have Christ in us and how that helps us to better follow Him

LIFE CHANGE

- to identify an area of our lives where acting on our faith is difficult
- to share our faith with one person with whom we have never shared it
- set aside time to call one person who needs encouragement

Icebreaker

10-15 minutes

**GATHERING
THE PEOPLE
◡ Form
horseshoe
groups of
6–8 people.**

It's a Mystery to Me! Go around the group on question 1 and let everyone share. Then go around again on questions 2 and 3, as time allows.

1. How does reading or watching mysteries make you feel?

   ☐ Stimulated—I always like to see if I can solve it before the detective.
   ☐ Excited—I get wrapped up in the story.
   ☐ Okay—but I prefer romances.
   ☐ Depends on if anything gets blown up.
   ☐ Bored—it's always the same formula stuff.
   ☐ I just go to the last page first.
   ☐ other: _____

2. To what real-life mystery would you most like to know the answer?

   ☐ What really happened when JFK was killed?
   ☐ Is the government actually hiding evidence of UFOs?
   ☐ What happens to all those socks I lose so I wind up with half a pair?
   ☐ Why does it always rain when I plan the picnic?

☐ What is behind the disappearances in the Bermuda Triangle?
☐ Did OJ really do it?
☐ What do women want—really?
☐ Why are men so clueless?
☐ other: _____

3. If your life were a mystery book, how would you title it?

Bible Study

30-45 minutes **4**

The Scripture for this week:

²⁴*Now I rejoice in my sufferings for you, and I am completing in my flesh what is lacking in Christ's afflictions for His body, that is, the church.* ²⁵*I have become its minister, according to God's administration that was given to me for you, to make God's message fully known,* ²⁶*the mystery hidden for ages and generations but now revealed to His saints.* ²⁷*God wanted to make known to those among the Gentiles the glorious wealth of this mystery, which is Christ in you, the hope of glory.* ²⁸*We proclaim Him, warning and teaching everyone with all wisdom, so that we may present everyone mature in Christ.* ²⁹*I labor for this, striving with His strength that works powerfully in me.*

¹*For I want you to know how great a struggle I have for you, for those in Laodicea, and for all who have not seen me in person.* ²*I want their hearts to be encouraged and joined together in love, so that they may have all the riches of assured understanding, and have the knowledge of God's mystery—Christ.* ³*In Him all the treasures of wisdom and knowledge are hidden.*

⁴*I am saying this so that no one will deceive you with persuasive arguments.* ⁵*For I may be absent in body, but I am with you in spirit, rejoicing to see your good order and the strength of your faith in Christ.*

...about today's session

1. What did all of the Greek mystery religions essentially teach?

2. To whom did Paul say the "mystery" of Christ in us was available?

3. What did old-line Judaism and the Greek mystery religions have in common in their teachings?

Identifying with the Story

1. What have you labored for with the same energy that Paul had as he labored for his churches?

2. When do you remember getting a sense of fulfillment from serving someone else? What made this act of service fulfilling? In what ways were your feelings similar to Paul's?

3. Whose heart do you feel the need to encourage? Why is that person in extra need of encouragement?

today's session

1. Paul saw himself as called to fill what three roles?

_____

_____

_____

2. In what way did Paul's suffering "complete" the suffering of Christ?

3. What two things did Paul do regularly to encourage believers?

_____

_____

4. What two sources of pressure on early Christians made it especially important that they receive encouragement?

_____

_____

4

5. In what ways might Christians of today have to suffer because of their faith?

Learning from the Story

♘ **In horseshoe groups of 6-8, choose an answer and explain why you chose what you did.**

1. Have you ever suffered for your faith? In what way? What does this passage say to you about that experience?

2. What "persuasive arguments" have you heard that pull people away from their hope in Jesus Christ? Which of these, if any, have given you the most trouble?

3. What does it mean to you to have "Christ in you" at this point in your life? What do you need to do to keep yourself aware of His presence and strength within you?

life change lessons

1. Who comes to mind when you think of people who have suffered for their faith? Does their example encourage you to do the same or make you think they are somehow stronger and better than you could ever be?

2. Where does the power for doing things like suffering for our faith come from?

Caring Time

15-20 minutes

Close by taking time to pray for one another and for your own special concerns. Begin by having each group member answer this question:

"In what area of your life do you need some encouragement this week?"

Pray for these needs, as well as the concerns on the Prayer/Praise Report. Include prayer that God would guide you to someone to invite for next week to fill the empty chair.

Reference Notes

Use these notes to gain further understanding of the text as you study on your own.

completing in my flesh what is lacking in Christ's afflictions. Given Paul's stress on the once-for-all sufficiency of Christ's death as a sacrifice for sin (1:22), he could not mean that his sufferings somehow added to the value of Christ's death. Some believe he was alluding to Jewish apocalyptic tradition that anticipated a definite series of catastrophic events that must be experienced before the Messiah establishes the new world order. Since these events were related to the Messiah's appearance, they were known as the "woes of the Messiah."

to make God's message fully known. This is another reminder that the gospel they have heard is indeed the complete gospel. There is nothing lacking that the false teachers can "fulfill."

the mystery ... now revealed. These words may be allusions to Greek mystery religions that were popular at the time. Paul may have been using their language to show that the gospel is a better "mystery" than what they had been teaching. Such language could also have been borrowed from Jewish apocalyptic literature, which spoke of God's hidden mysteries whose meanings were revealed to only a few. God reveals the "mystery" of the gospel to all—including Gentiles—who believe. It is not a secret form of spiritual power, but the hope for eternity guaranteed by the presence of Christ within the believer.

mature in Christ. The gospel message, which begins, continues, and ends with obeying Christ, is for all types of people who come to spiritual maturity through their day-to-day allegiance to Christ.

Laodicea. A city located a short distance from Colossae (4:16).

4

encouraged and joined together in love. The false teachers said there was a secret knowledge gained only by those few who practiced a variety of rites, experiences, or disciplines. Such a spirituality would naturally tend to discourage people and lead to factions. In contrast to such spiritual elitism, the gospel views spiritual growth as a growth in love for Christ and one another. This would lead to hope and shared fellowship.

notes

5

Nail It!

Prepare for the Session

	READINGS	REFLECTIVE QUESTIONS
Monday	Colossians 2:6-7	In what way has your faith been strengthened since starting this course?
Tuesday	Colossians 2:8-12	How susceptible are you to false and dangerous philosophies? How can you be less susceptible?
Wednesday	Colossians 2:13-15	Which sins or trespasses make you especially thankful that God has forgiven you? How can you show your thanks?
Thursday	Matthew 21:1-11	How was the triumphal entry of Christ into Jerusalem different from what the world calls triumph? How are you proclaiming Christ as King?
Friday	1 Corinthians 15:54-57	Have you let Christ have the victory over your own fear of death? Why or why not?
Saturday	1 John 5:4	What challenges in the world has your faith helped you overcome? What aspects of the world do you need more faith to master? How can Christ help you claim victory?
Sunday	Revelation 19:11-16	What will it mean when Christ truly reigns throughout the earth? What are you called to do to help?

5

BIBLE STUDY

- to fully understand the nature of the triumph we have through the cross of Christ
- to see the danger of false teaching and how it can rob us of our victory
- to discuss Christ's victory over spiritual powers and authorities

LIFE CHANGE

- to strengthen our commitment to regular personal Bible study
- to learn about and evaluate a competing philosophy
- to hold a personal forgiveness ceremony

Icebreaker

10-15 minutes

GATHERING THE PEOPLE
U Form horseshoe groups of 6–8 people.

Great Victories. Go around the group on question 1 and let everyone share. Then go around again on questions 2 and 3, as time allows.

1. What would you consider to be the greatest victory of your childhood or adolescence?

   ☐ learning to ride my bike
   ☐ beating out a rival for a certain guy or girl
   ☐ my sports team winning an important tournament
   ☐ getting cast for the role I wanted in a play or musical
   ☐ receiving an award for my music or art
   ☐ graduating from high school
   ☐ finally winning an argument with my parents
   ☐ receiving an important scholarship
   ☐ other: _____

2. If you could be assured of one victory in the coming year, what would you want it to be?

   ☐ to win "the battle of the bulge" and lose that extra weight
   ☐ to finally get the job I've been wanting
   ☐ to win a big contract I've been after
   ☐ to overcome an addiction

☐ to win the heart of a rebellious child
☐ to get a political leader I support elected
☐ to win an argument with my spouse
☐ to gain control of my finances
☐ other: _____

3. Seeing your life in terms of a game you really want to win, where do you feel you are right now in the contest?

☐ I'm way behind, with little or no chance of catching up.
☐ I think there's a big "L" on my forehead.
☐ I'm behind, but with hope of at least evening the score.
☐ I'm winning about as much as I'm losing.
☐ I'm ahead, but having to fight to stay that way.
☐ I'm way ahead, and cruising to the finish line.

Bible Study

30-45 minutes

5

The Scripture for this week:

LEARNING FROM THE BIBLE

COLOSSIANS 2:6–15

[6]Therefore as you have received Christ Jesus the Lord, walk in Him, [7]rooted and built up in Him and established in the faith, just as you were taught, and overflowing with thankfulness.

[8]Be careful that no one takes you captive through philosophy and empty deceit based on human tradition, based on the elemental forces of the world, and not based on Christ. [9]For in Him the entire fullness of God's nature dwells bodily, [10]and you have been filled by Him, who is the head over every ruler and authority. [11]In Him you were also circumcised with a circumcision not done with hands, by putting off the body of flesh, in the circumcision of the Messiah. [12]Having been buried with Him in baptism, you were also raised with Him through faith in the working of God, who raised Him from the dead. [13]And when you were dead in trespasses and in the uncircumcision of your flesh, He made you alive with Him and forgave us all our trespasses. [14]He erased the certificate of debt, with its obligations, that was against us and opposed to us, and has taken it out of the way by nailing it to the cross. [15]He disarmed the rulers and authorities and disgraced them publicly; He triumphed over them by Him.

...about today's session

1. How is the victory we have in Jesus Christ different from competitive victories in sports?

2. What three forces did Paul fight against in his time?

   _____

   _____

   _____

3. How is what we fight against today similar to what Paul fought against?

Identifying with the Story

1. When have you been taken "captive" by something or someone that, in the end, was deceitful?

2. When has being forgiven by someone given you a sense of freedom from captivity?

3. When have you felt the oppressiveness of debt? How is spiritual debt like financial debt? Which do you find more oppressive?

today's session

What is God teaching you from this story?

1. Over what three kinds of enemies can we triumph if we stick to the gospel we have been taught?

   1. _____

   2. _____

   3. _____

2. What two modern false teachings are mentioned? Can you think of others?

   _____

   _____

3. What connection does Scripture make between sin and death?

5

4. What historical event in the spiritual or unseen realm indicates that the "rulers and authorities" Paul wrote about were not human rulers and authorities?

Learning from the Story

◡ **In horseshoe groups of 6-8, choose an answer and explain why you chose what you did.**

1. What causes people to turn away from the faith they are taught? How can Christians help each other become more firmly "rooted" and "established in the faith" (v. 7) so this is less likely to happen?

2. What does it mean to be "dead in trespasses" (v. 13)? How does Christ help make us alive again?

3. What evidence, if any, have you seen of evil spiritual "rulers and authorities"? What does it mean to you that such powers have been "disarmed" and "disgraced" (v. 15)?

life change lessons

1. What victories has God won in your life? What victories does He still need to win?

2. What debts did you owe before Christ paid them at the cross?

Caring Time

15-20 minutes

Remember that this time is for developing and expressing your caring for each other. Since we are called by our passage to be "overflowing with thankfulness" (v. 7), let's be in that spirit! Begin by having each group member answer this question:

"What are some victories God has given you for which you are especially thankful?"

Thank God for these victories, and then move on to praying for the concerns on the Prayer/Praise Report. Pray specifically for God to guide you to someone to bring next week to fill the empty chair.

Reference Notes

Use these notes to gain further understanding
of the text as you study on your own.

**COLOSSIANS
2:6**

received Christ Jesus the Lord. To receive Jesus as "Lord" is to acknowledge Him as the supreme authority in one's life.

**COLOSSIANS
2:8**

philosophy and empty deceit. The false teachings were not based on the
teachings of Christ, but upon faulty ideas influenced by the "basic principles" of the world, angelic beings that manipulated human affairs in oppo-
sition to God (1:16; 1 Cor. 2:6,8; Gal. 3:19; 4:3,9; Eph. 6:12).

**COLOSSIANS
2:9**

in Him the entire fullness of God's nature dwells bodily. While the
false teachers related to fallen angelic beings, believers relate to God
incarnate (1:19).

**COLOSSIANS
2:10**

you have been filled by Him. Believing in Christ, one needs to look
nowhere else for any greater spiritual power, knowledge, or experience.

**COLOSSIANS
2:11**

circumcised. The false teachers' ascetic route to spiritual fulfillment
included circumcision. This circumcision was probably not based on the
Old Testament circumcision as a sign of obedience to the Law of Moses
(Gal. 5:2-4), but on the Greek mystery religions that practiced circumcision as a symbol of being emancipated from the fleshly limits of the body
in order to enter the realm of spiritual reality.

**COLOSSIANS
2:13**

when you were dead. Jesus' physical death is compared with the lack of
spiritual life in the Colossians prior to their conversion (Eph. 2:1-10).
uncircumcision. Paul countered that a physical act will not cure the
problem of a *heart* that is not set apart for God. This is the same argument
used in the Old Testament to call Jews to circumcise their hearts for God
(Deut. 10:16; Jer. 4:4).

**COLOSSIANS
2:14**

the certificate of debt. This refers to a written agreement to pay back a
debt or to obey a law. When fulfilled, the document was blotted out and
canceled.

**COLOSSIANS
2:15**

triumphed over. Paul used the image of a conquering hero forcing the
vanquished army to march after him in a victory parade.

notes

Session

6

Transformational Flow Chart

Prepare for the Session

	READINGS	REFLECTIVE QUESTIONS
Monday	Colossians 2:16-19	On what matters are you letting others judge you? What would Christ say about this?
Tuesday	Colossians 2:20-23	In what ways are you letting yourself be tied up by regulations? How would Christ free you?
Wednesday	John 15:1-4	How is your connection to Christ resulting in your life "bearing fruit"?
Thursday	John 15:5-6	At what point(s) in your life have you found yourself withering away in isolation?
Friday	1 Corinthians 12:12-13	How does remaining connected to Christ, the Head, solidify your fellowship with others in the body, the church?
Saturday	1 Corinthians 12:27-30	How are you currently serving Christ with your gifts?
Sunday	Hebrews 10:24-25	What role does attendance at worship and other church events play in keeping you connected to Christ?

49

BIBLE STUDY
- to understand that Christ is the Head of the church and of each individual member
- to consider the role of ascetic practices in Christian living
- to evaluate the role negative rules play in how we are to act and live as Christians

LIFE CHANGE
- to evaluate who in our lives is pulling our guilt strings
- to make this week's decisions with greater deliberation
- to begin each day with a spiritual "Pledge of Allegiance"

Icebreaker
10-15 minutes

GATHERING
THE PEOPLE
◡ Form
horseshoe
groups of
6–8 people.

The Big "Don'ts" of Life. Go around the group on question 1 and let everyone share. Then go around again on questions 2 and 3, as time allows.

1. With which of the following "don'ts" did you have the hardest time when you were a child or adolescent?

   ☐ "Don't drink milk or juice right out of the carton!"
   ☐ "Don't talk with your mouth full!"
   ☐ "Don't talk back to your mother/father!"
   ☐ "Don't eat in the living room!"
   ☐ "Don't play that music so loud!"
   ☐ "Don't have friends over while we're gone!"
   ☐ "Don't talk to strangers!"
   ☐ "Don't pet stray dogs!"

2. Which of the following "do's and don'ts" best exemplifies the philosophy of the home where you were raised?

   ☐ "Don't do anything I wouldn't do."
   ☐ "Do unto others as you would have them do unto you."
   ☐ "Do unto others BEFORE they do unto you."
   ☐ "Do whatever you want, but don't get caught."
   ☐ "Don't get mad—get even."   ☐ "If in doubt—don't."
   ☐ "Don't ask—don't tell."   ☐ "Do your best."

3. If you had to choose one "don't" that you wish people today would observe more closely, what would it be?

Bible Study

30-45 minutes

The Scripture for this week:

[16]*Therefore don't let anyone judge you in regard to food and drink or in the matter of a festival or a new moon or a sabbath day.* [17]*These are a shadow of what was to come; the substance is the Messiah.* [18]*Let no one disqualify you, insisting on ascetic practices and the worship of angels, claiming access to a visionary realm and inflated without cause by his fleshly mind.* [19]*He doesn't hold on to the Head, from whom the whole body, nourished and held together by its ligaments and tendons, develops with growth from God.*

[20]*If you died with Christ to the elemental forces of this world, why do you live as if you still belonged to the world? Why do you submit to regulations:* [21]*"Don't handle, don't taste, don't touch"?* [22]*All these regulations refer to what is destroyed by being used up; they are human commands and doctrines.* [23]*Although these have a reputation of wisdom by promoting ascetic practices, humility, and severe treatment of the body, they are not of any value against fleshly indulgence.*

...about today's session

**A WORD
FROM THE
LEADER**

1. To what does failing to keep in touch with Christ as Head lead?

**Write your
answers
here.**

2. What happens to the physical body when the neurological pathways to the brain are compromised? What are the implications when this dynamic occurs relative to a Christian or a church body?

3. If we split the role of "head" of our lives between Christ and anyone else, what can happen?

Identifying with the Story

⊍ In
horseshoe
groups of 6–8,
explore
questions as
time allows.

1. In what area of behavior do you feel others are most likely to judge you?

   ☐ what I eat or drink
   ☐ my appearance—whether or not I'm "attractive," overweight, too thin, etc.
   ☐ my fashion sense—styles like earrings, tattoos, hair coloring, etc.
   ☐ my friends
   ☐ the movies or television shows I watch
   ☐ my political involvement
   ☐ other: _____

2. When you feel others are judging you, how are you most likely to react?

   ☐ I judge them in return.
   ☐ I shrug it off.
   ☐ I act even more eccentric.
   ☐ I fly into a rage.
   ☐ I try to be like they want me to be.
   ☐ I take it to God in prayer.
   ☐ I find out what my friends think.
   ☐ other: _____

3. If Christ could say one thing to you about the way you are relating to the judgments and regulations others try to place upon you, what do you think He would say?

today's session

What is God teaching you from this story?

1. Can a person "take charge of his or her life" and have Christ as Head? What happens when we try to take charge of our lives without including Christ?

2. What two problems result when we don't make Christ the undisputed Head of our lives?

 ____

 ____

3. Why is normal guilt vital to healthy functioning as an adult?

4. Upon what philosopher is Paul's language about shadow and substance based? For Paul, what is the "shadow," and what is the "substance"?

6

5. What was the difference between Paul's teachings about ascetic practices, and what the mystery religions of Colossae seemed to be teaching?

Learning from the Story

In horseshoe groups of 6-8, choose an answer and explain why you chose what you did.

1. What does it mean to "live as if you still belonged to the world" (v. 20)? To whom do we belong?

2. Why are people so prone to get tied up in the "don'ts" of life? To what degree are the "don'ts" helpful, and to what degree are they insufficient?

3. What practices and attitudes have you found most helpful in restraining yourself from "fleshly indulgence" (overeating, addictive behavior, etc.)? How has Christ helped you?

life change lessons

How can you apply this session to your life?

1. What must we do to develop an action plan for an abstract goal like keeping Christ as Head of our lives?

Write your answers here.

2. As we begin each day, what can we do to help keep Christ as our Head?

Caring Time
15-20 minutes

CARING TIME

Close by praying for one another. Begin this time by having each group member answer this question:

☾ Remain in horseshoe groups of 6-8.

"What issue are you facing in the coming week for which you will need Christ's direction, as Head of your life?"

Pray for Christ's direction on these issues, and then move on to praying for the concerns on the Prayer/Praise Report. Continue to pray for God's guidance on whom to invite to fill the empty chair.

Reference Notes

Use these notes to gain further understanding
of the text as you study on your own.

**COLOSSIANS
2:16**

eat or drink. Ascetic practices were common in ancient religions. In this context, the reason for such practices appears to have been to attune oneself to the "elemental spirits" that controlled the world.

a festival or a new moon or a sabbath day. These events serve as a summary of the annual, monthly, and weekly Jewish holy days (1 Chron. 23:31). Pagans also observed cycles of worship determined by astrological practices. The false teachers probably used the Jewish traditions to support their astrological calendar.

**COLOSSIANS
2:17**

a shadow ... the substance. Hebrews 8:3-13 and 10:1-18 use this Platonic imagery to describe the work of Christ as compared to the Old Testament sacrificial system (see also 1 Cor. 5:7). While the false teachers claimed their ascetic practices were the pathway that led to the reality of spiritual experience, Paul asserted that they only lead to the shadowlands and not to a true spiritual life.

**COLOSSIANS
2:18**

ascetic practices. Paul was obviously not repudiating a true humility before God, but rather had in mind the ascetic practices, like enforced fasting, which mask pride with a facade of humility.

worship of angels. Since there is little evidence of a cult of angels at this time, the false teachers may have claimed their spiritual elevation allowed them to worship the Deity in the company of the angels.

access to a visionary realm. Inscriptions in pagan temples used this phrase to refer to a rite that authorized a person to be a teacher of the divine mysteries.

**COLOSSIANS
2:19**

the Head. Having abandoned Christ as their authority, the false teachers were not part of the body (the church).

**COLOSSIANS
2:20**

died with Christ. Elsewhere, Paul used the image of dying with Christ to show how the believer's bond to sin (Rom. 6:16-18,23) and to the Law (Rom. 7:1,4) is broken. Here, he used it to show that their bondage to the "elemental forces" had also been severed. Since the power of the forces has been severed, it is foolish to submit to their authority as a route to spiritual life (Gal. 4:1-11).

**COLOSSIANS
2:23**

promoting ascetic practices. The problem here is not ascetic practices as spiritual disciplines. Jesus himself fasted in the wilderness for 40 days. The problem seems to be that there were those in Colossae who taught that such practices were necessary for salvation. This emphasis then replaced their reliance on Christ.

notes

7

Phenomenal Focus

Prepare for the Session

	READINGS	REFLECTIVE QUESTIONS
Monday	Colossians 3:1	What attitude taught by your parents do you need to reaffirm?
Tuesday	Colossians 3:2-4	On what is your mind usually focused—on the heavenly or the earthly? How can you focus more on "what is above"?
Wednesday	Colossians 3:5	What worldly passions do you struggle with the most? What needs to happen for you to have a victory over these passions?
Thursday	Colossians 3:6-7	What moral issues that tempted you once has Christ helped you overcome? Have you thanked Him for these victories?
Friday	Matthew 6:19-21	What is your "investment strategy" for investing in things that are eternal?
Saturday	Matthew 16:21-23	How is your mind's focal point reflected in your attitude toward suffering and death?
Sunday	1 Corinthians 9:24-25	Are you "running the race" for a heavenly prize or an earthly one? What does this imply for how you discipline yourself?

7

BIBLE STUDY
- to understand the importance of focusing on spiritual values rather than worldly ones
- to consider what it means to die to self and come alive to Christ, and how this can help us deal with temptations
- to realize the value of setting spiritual goals to let Christ truly control our lives

LIFE CHANGE
- to compose a personal life mission statement
- to define life goals for the next five years
- to set two to three objectives for each life goal for the next five years

Icebreaker
10-15 minutes

GATHERING
THE PEOPLE
U Form
horseshoe
groups of
6–8 people.

Parental Wrath. Go around the group on question 1 and let everyone share. Then go around again on questions 2 and 3, as time allows.

1. When you were a child, which of the following would have been most likely to stir up your parents' wrath against you?

   ☐ talking back to them   ☐ lying
   ☐ not getting my chores done   ☐ making a mess
   ☐ making too much noise   ☐ other: _____
   ☐ playing, fighting, or rough-housing indoors
   ☐ inviting friends over without asking
   ☐ watching TV instead of doing homework

2. Which of the following images best describes how your parents expressed their anger? Put an "M" by the answer for your mother and an "F" by the answer for your father.

   ____ like a volcano—dormant for long periods, then exploding without warning
   ____ like a wounded grizzly bear—destroying all in its wake
   ____ like a mama lion—using a few well-placed growls and swats
   ____ like an angry bird—chirping and fluttering all over the place, but doing little damage

_____ like an angry house cat—stay out of his way and you're okay, but get too close and you get your face sliced

_____ like an injured bunny—quietly hiding away in some corner of the cage

3. What more than anything else incites you to wrath as an adult?

Bible Study
30-45 minutes

The Scripture for this week:

LEARNING
FROM THE
BIBLE

COLOSSIANS
3:1-7

¹So if you have been raised with the Messiah, seek what is above, where the Messiah is, seated at the right hand of God. ²Set your minds on what is above, not on what is on the earth. ³For you have died, and your life is hidden with the Messiah in God. ⁴When the Messiah, who is your life, is revealed, then you also will be revealed with Him in glory.

⁵Therefore, put to death whatever in you is worldly: sexual immorality, impurity, lust, evil desire, and greed, which is idolatry. ⁶Because of these, God's wrath comes on the disobedient, ⁷and you once walked in these things when you were living in them.

7

...about today's session

**A WORD
FROM THE
LEADER**

1. Why is it important to go beyond the generalities to the specifics of what Christ calls us to do and not do?

**Write your
answers
here.**

2. What societal influences are mentioned as making it harder to follow what Christ wants? What in our society makes it harder for you to live up to the specific behavioral demands of Jesus Christ?

3. How does society's attitude toward greed contrast to that of Christ?

Identifying with the Story

◖ In
horseshoe
groups of 6–8,
explore
questions as
time allows.

1. Which of the following statements best expresses the attitude toward Christ with which you were raised?

☐ He was at the center of our family's life.
☐ We relied on Him to pull us through in hard times.
☐ We sought to honor and obey Him.
☐ We paid homage to Him at Easter and Christmas.
☐ He was one we knew about, but mostly ignored.
☐ We rejected Him.
☐ His name was mostly mentioned in our swearing.

2. Were you to leave this earthly life today what, besides people, would you have the hardest time leaving behind?

3. When it comes to focusing your life on Christ instead of earthly things, in which of the following circumstances do you have the hardest time?

☐ when I'm in a shopping mall   ☐ pretty much always
☐ when I see what my neighbors or coworkers have
☐ when I'm where there are a lot of attractive people of the opposite sex
☐ when I'm watching commercials on TV
☐ when I'm visiting someone else's really nice home
☐ pretty much always
☐ other: _____

today's session

1. What does Paul teach here regarding wrong attitudes? How does that compare to what Jesus taught about such things?

2. What does it mean to "die to self"?

3. How does the presence of Christ within us help with attitudes like lust and greed?

4. What does "setting our minds on what is above" imply for setting life goals?

5. What three areas of our lives might spiritual goals include?

_____

_____

_____

Learning from the Story

7

↻ In horseshoe groups of 6-8, choose an answer and explain why you chose what you did.

1. What does it mean to you that your life is "hidden with the Messiah in God" (v. 3)? How does this help with temptation?

2. What do you now see as the most important weapon you have in your arsenal to deal a "death blow" to the behaviors and attitudes Paul refers to here: sexual immorality, impurity, lust, evil desire, and greed?

3. If greed is "idolatry," what or who would Christ say you are truly worshiping right now? Are you making yourself susceptible to receiving God's wrath?

life change lessons

How can you apply this session to your life?

Write your answers here.

1. What are the elements of long-term planning?

2. How should a Christian prepare for writing a life mission statement?

Caring Time

15-20 minutes

CARING TIME

♘ Remain in horseshoe groups of 6-8.

Take time now to care for one another through prayer. Today we want to care for each other by supporting the process of overcoming temptation. Begin by having each group member finish this sentence:

> *"The 'evil desire' I am having the most*
> *difficulty with right now is ..."*

Pray for the strength and presence of Christ to give you the victory over these desires. Then move on to praying for the concerns on the Prayer/Praise Report.

Pray specifically for God to guide you to someone to invite for next week to fill the empty chair.

BIBLE STUDY NOTES

Reference Notes

Use these notes to gain further understanding
of the text as you study on your own.

COLOSSIANS 3:1

raised with the Messiah. As the Christian's death-with-Christ cut the bonds to the old authorities (2:20), so one's life-with-Christ creates new bonds with God and others. "Messiah" is the Hebrew equivalent of the Greek word "Christ."

COLOSSIANS
3:1
(cont'd)

seek what is above. This is not encouraging escapism from earthly affairs. The point is that Christians are to shape their lives by the values of the heavenly world in which Christ sits enthroned as King, rather than heeding rules based on the elemental spirits.

COLOSSIANS
3:3

hidden with the Messiah in God. Why might a person's life need to be "hidden"? The allusion is to protection. In Exodus 33:22, God tells Moses that he will hide him in the cleft of a rock while His glory passes by. The sin-infected Moses needed to be protected from the glory of the sinless God, because sinful man cannot see God and live. Jesus is the "rock" in which we "hide" to protect us from the judgment of a righteous God. This is particularly relevant because the passage later refers to the wrath of God coming to judge evil behavior and attitudes (v. 6).

COLOSSIANS
3:5

put to death. Believers are to daily turn away from attitudes and actions that reflect the old way of life. *worldly.* Worldly attitudes and behaviors disregard God and follow selfish desires.
greed, which is idolatry. Jewish teachers frequently identified greed with idolatry. Paul says in 1 Timothy 6:10, "For the love of money is a root of all kinds of evil, and by craving it, some have wandered away from the faith and pierced themselves with many pains."

COLOSSIANS
3:7

you once walked in these things. Paul was writing to Greeks who had lived in a society that was relatively unrestrained in terms of sexual morals. Paul similarly warns the Christians of Corinth not to go back to their former licentious ways in 1 Corinthians 6:9-11. He knew that backsliding is a constant danger for a reformed life, as many in AA and other modern addiction groups have also learned.

7

notes

Managing Mad

Prepare for the Session

	READINGS	REFLECTIVE QUESTIONS
Monday	Colossians 3:8	Does your everyday language reflect the Lord you serve?
Tuesday	Colossians 3:9-10	When was the last time you lied to someone you cared about? How could you have dealt with the situation more honestly?
Wednesday	Colossians 3:11	What cultural differences are you allowing to separate you from others who are part of Christ's body?
Thursday	2 Corinthians 5:17	In what ways have you become someone new since you gave your life to Christ?
Friday	Ephesians 4:22-24	What have you done to change your "former way of life" and the harmful behaviors that were part of your pre-Christ life?
Saturday	Ephesians 4:25	Are you part of a Christian community where you can truly be honest with each other? What can you do to make truth and honesty more a part of your new way of being?
Sunday	Ephesians 4:26-27	Are you able to express your anger without sinning and deliberately hurting others?

BIBLE STUDY

- to consider how a person who seeks to be a new person in Christ should handle anger
- to understand the importance of truth and honesty in the Christian community
- to affirm the need to break down walls between people of different cultures

LIFE CHANGE

- to keep an "anger diary" for a week and observe how we deal with anger
- to confidentially reveal something personal to a trusted friend
- to become better acquainted with a Christian of another race or culture

Icebreaker

10-15 minutes

GATHERING THE PEOPLE
◟ Form horseshoe groups of 6–8 people.

Liar, Liar, Pants on Fire! Go around the group on question 1 and let everyone share. Then go around again on questions 2 and 3, as time allows.

1. Which of the following lies do you remember your parents catching you in when you were a teen?

   ☐ "Party while you were gone? What party?"
   ☐ "Sure, I've finished my homework."
   ☐ "Yes, there will be parental supervision."
   ☐ "I'm just going to the library."
   ☐ "That smell of cigarettes?—It must have been from the people around me."
   ☐ "How should I know who broke it?"
   ☐ "All of the other parents are letting their kids do it."
   ☐ "I have no idea who brought those filthy magazines into the house!"

2. Which of the following lies do you find yourself telling most frequently today?

   ☐ "The check is in the mail."   ☐ "Of course I trust you!"
   ☐ "Sure I liked it. I'm just full."   ☐ "Angry? I'm not angry!"

☐ "Sure! That dress looks great on you!"
☐ "You should have seen the one that got away!"
☐ "Why, I've never even looked at another man/woman!"

3. What kind of liar would you say you are?

☐ Terrible!—I always give it away in my eyes or voice.
☐ Really bad—I feel guilty until I confess.
☐ Okay—I can do it when I feel I have to.
☐ Pretty good actually—I can get by with most lies I tell.
☐ Pathological—I sometimes lie for no reason at all!
☐ other: _____

Bible Study
30-45 minutes

The Scripture for this week:

LEARNING FROM THE BIBLE

COLOSSIANS 3:8–11

⁸But now you must also put away all the following: anger, wrath, malice, slander, and filthy language from your mouth. ⁹Do not lie to one another, since you have put off the old man with his practices ¹⁰and have put on the new man, who is being renewed in knowledge according to the image of his Creator. ¹¹Here there is not Greek and Jew, circumcision and uncircumcision, barbarian, Scythian, slave and free; but Christ is all and in all.

8

...about today's session

A WORD FROM THE LEADER

Write your answers here.

1. What overall goal does this passage give us for our spiritual growth?

2. What is the problem with first seeing what we achieve and then claiming that was our goal all along?

3. What are three behavioral "targets" that God sets before us through this passage?

_____

_____

_____

Identifying with the Story

1. In which of the following ways are you most likely to express your anger?

☐ I'm a yeller.
☐ I hit and throw things—be sure to duck!
☐ You don't want to hear the words I use.
☐ I generally just talk it out.
☐ I go running or take it out on the tennis court.
☐ I get back at the one I'm angry at.
☐ I try not to think about it.
☐ I just seethe and quietly hold on to my anger for days.
☐ other: _____

2. Finish this sentence: "The one thing I most wish I could change about the way I express my anger is ..."

3. To whom do you have the hardest time telling the truth?

☐ my friends—I don't want to hurt their feelings.
☐ my spouse or significant other—If I told him/her the truth, they would get mad.
☐ customers—I need their business.
☐ the government—They expect it.
☐ strangers I do business with—It's not like I really care about them.
☐ my parents—They just wouldn't understand.
☐ other: _____

What is God teaching you from this story?

1. What are three essential "job qualifications" for the new self in Jesus Christ?

   _____

   _____

   _____

2. What are two examples of Jesus getting angry?

   _____

   _____

3. What are two ways to mismanage anger?

   _____

   _____

4. In what ways did Jesus set an example for us by being truthful with His disciples?

5. What are some of the divisions between people that Christ can help us heal?

8

Learning from the Story

In horseshoe groups of 6-8, choose an answer and explain why you chose what you did.

1. Which of the following would you consider to be "filthy" language? Which is most offensive to you?

   ☐ language with bathroom references
   ☐ language with slang sexual references
   ☐ language that takes God's name in vain
   ☐ language that is hateful to another race or culture
   ☐ language that puts others down

2. What reason is given for why we should not lie to one another (vv. 9-10)? Why should this be a deterrent to lying?

3. Had Paul been writing today, what groups might he have included in verse 11? What can Christians do to help bring such groups together?

life change lessons

**How can you
apply this
session to
your life?**

**Write your
answers
here.**

1. What are three important traits that our text adds to our "new-self shopping list"?

_____

_____

_____

2. What is God's "financing plan" for getting a new self?

Caring Time

15-20 minutes

Take this time to encourage and care for one another in prayer. Today we want to care for each other by sharing some of the things that are irritating us and which we need to get off our chest. Begin by finishing this sentence:

"Right now, I am feeling most angry about ..."

Pray for the strength and understanding to deal with these anger issues. Then move on to praying for the concerns on the Prayer/Praise Report.

Pray specifically for God to guide you to someone to invite for next week to fill the empty chair.

Reference Notes

Use these notes to gain further understanding
of the text as you study on your own.

**BIBLE
STUDY
NOTES**

**COLOSSIANS
3:8**

anger, wrath. The Greek word translated "anger" most often refers to a sudden flare of temper, while the Greek word for "wrath" most often refers to a lingering hostility.

filthy language. The implication here may actually be closer to "abusive language."

**COLOSSIANS
3:9**

put off the old man. Literally, "to strip off." This phrase is also used to describe the putting off of the sinful nature through Christ's death (2:11), and Christ's victory over spiritual powers (2:15).

**COLOSSIANS
3:10**

put on the new man. The lifestyle of Christians is patterned after the attitudes and actions of Christ who is at work within them (1 Cor. 15:45; Gal. 3:27).

according to the image of his Creator. In this letter we have already read that "the image of the invisible God" is Jesus Christ (1:15). So to be formed in the image of our Creator is also to be conformed to Jesus Christ.

**COLOSSIANS
3:11**

Scythian. The Greeks considered Scythians to be especially uncouth barbarians. Allegiance to Christ eradicates prideful divisions based on race, religion, culture, or social class (and gender—Gal. 3:28).

8

notes

Session

9

Unmistakable Unanimity

Prepare for the Session

	READINGS	REFLECTIVE QUESTIONS
Monday	Colossians 3:12-13	Whom do you need to forgive today?
Tuesday	Colossians 3:14-15	When was the last time you felt "a perfect bond of unity" with the people around you? What was it that helped you to feel this way?
Wednesday	Colossians 3:16-17	What are you doing to celebrate all that Christ has done for you? Can those around you tell how thankful you are?
Thursday	Romans 2:23-24	What have you done recently that reflected poorly on your witness for Christ? Is there anything you might do to counteract this negative witness?
Friday	Matthew 18:21-35	How can your forgiveness toward others serve as a witness to what Christ has done for you?
Saturday	Matthew 10:40-42	What act of kindness can you do this week in the name of Jesus?
Sunday	John 20:21-23	Are you busy doing what Christ has sent you out to do?

9

BIBLE STUDY
- to understand more fully the role of loving others in our Christian walk
- to appreciate the need for Christian unity in witnessing to Christ
- to see why thanking God is essential to honoring the name of Christ

LIFE CHANGE
- to do one "servant task" around our home that we are not used to doing
- to forgive one person we have had conflict with in the church
- to make a list of all we have to be thankful for

Icebreaker

10-15 minutes

**GATHERING
THE PEOPLE
U Form
horseshoe
groups of
6–8 people.**

Peace Signs. Go around the group on question 1 and let everyone share. Then go around again on questions 2 and 3, as time allows.

1. Where are you most likely to go when you are seeking a little peace in your life?

☐ out in my car for a drive
☐ my office with the phones on silent ring
☐ a favorite retreat in the mountains or countryside
☐ to a special little park   ☐ my garden
☐ a favorite fishing hole   ☐ the golf course
☐ a chapel or sanctuary   ☐ I have no such place.
☐ The bathroom is my only refuge. ☐ other: _____

2. Which of the following descriptions of "peace" means the most to you?

☐ no deadlines to have to meet   ☐ meaningful activity
☐ a sense of accomplishment   ☐ a sense of belonging
☐ confidence in the future
☐ no painful memories to deal with
☐ nobody harassing me to do stuff I don't want to do
☐ a sense of oneness with the world and nature

3. What would make the most relevant "peace sign" for your life?

☐ a mountain—It speaks of the majesty of God.
☐ a rainbow—Peace has often come after my storms.
☐ the traditional peace sign—Peace in the world and peace within go hand in hand for me.
☐ a dove—It calms me and reminds me of the Holy Spirit.
☐ a beautiful sunrise—It speaks of the hope of tomorrow.
☐ the cross—Peace comes from the release of my guilt.
☐ other: _____

Bible Study

30-45 minutes

The Scripture for this week:

LEARNING FROM THE BIBLE

COLOSSIANS 3:12–17

[12]Therefore, God's chosen ones, holy and loved, put on heartfelt compassion, kindness, humility, gentleness, and patience, [13]accepting one another and forgiving one another if anyone has a complaint against another. Just as the Lord has forgiven you, so also you must forgive. [14]Above all, put on love—the perfect bond of unity. [15]And let the peace of the Messiah, to which you were also called in one body, control your hearts. Be thankful. [16]Let the message about the Messiah dwell richly among you, teaching and admonishing one another in all wisdom, and singing psalms, hymns, and spiritual songs, with gratitude in your hearts to God. [17]And whatever you do, in word or in deed, do everything in the name of the Lord Jesus, giving thanks to God the Father through Him.

9

...about today's session

A WORD FROM THE LEADER

Write your answers here.

1. What are four situations where we might be called upon to honor the name of a group we represent?

_____

_____

_____

_____

2. How is the way of Christ's follower to be different from the way of the world?

3. Why do people who try to exalt their own names often wind up empty?

Identifying with the Story

◡ In horseshoe groups of 6–8, explore questions as time allows.

1. Which of the qualities in verses 12-13 do you have the hardest time "putting on"?

   ☐ heartfelt compassion—feeling deeply the need of others
   ☐ kindness—doing little acts to help, with no expectation of anything in return
   ☐ humility—realizing it isn't all about me
   ☐ gentleness—showing sensitivity so as not to wound others
   ☐ patience—giving others time to change and grow
   ☐ forgiving others—not holding on to old grudges

2. How would you describe the "bond of unity" that exists in your church fellowship?

   ☐ Perfect—we are held together by the strength of God's love.
   ☐ Strong, though not perfect—like "super-glue."
   ☐ Uneven—some places are holding together better than others.
   ☐ Pulling apart—like hardened old glue.
   ☐ Not holding at all—like using flour paste on metal parts.

3. What "psalms, hymns, and spiritual songs" especially speak to you? What is there about these expressions that touches your heart or especially expresses what you feel toward God?

today's session

What is God teaching you from this story?

1. What are two ways that Jesus' name is abused today?

_____

_____

2. What six acts or qualities are part of what it means to love?

_____

_____

_____

_____

_____

_____

3. How is a biblical understanding of humility different from the one people often have in the world?

4. What is a common image that Paul used to tell Christians that they must act together in unity?

9

5. What two things happen when we decide to live a life of gratitude to God?

_____

_____

Learning from the Story

⊍ In horseshoe groups of 6-8, choose an answer and explain why you chose what you did.

1. What is the relationship between letting the peace of the Messiah rule in your heart and forming the attitudes listed in verses 12 and 13? What do you need to do to open your heart more to this peace?

2. Which of the following comes the closest to the meaning of the phrase, "Let the message about the Messiah dwell richly among you" (v. 16)?

   ☐ The gospel needs to be lived out in the church, not just taught.

   ☐ We need to find as many ways as we can to teach about Jesus.

   ☐ We need to feel the message as well as understand it.

   ☐ We need to discourage anything that would take our focus off of Christ.

3. What would you say is your biggest barrier to having a consistent attitude of thankfulness?

   ☐ I have a tendency to see the negative in life.

   ☐ I don't have much to be thankful for right now.

   ☐ It isn't the way I was raised.

   ☐ I'm caught up in our society's drive for more.

   ☐ I find no barriers—I'm full of thanksgiving right now!

   ☐ other: _____

life change lessons

How can you apply this session to your life?

Write your answers here.

1. What instances are mentioned that show popular culture's frustration about love and what it means? Can you think of others?

   _____

   _____

2. What have Christians already "gotten out" of love?

_____

_____

_____

Caring Time
15-20 minutes

◯ Remain in horseshoe groups of 6-8.

Use this time to pray and care for one another. Today we will begin by sharing things we are thankful for in regard to what has been happening in our group. Take turns having each group member answer the question:

"What has happened in this group for which you are most thankful to God?"

Thank God for all that people share. Then move on to praying for the concerns on the Prayer/Praise Report. Remember to include prayer for the empty chair.

Close by singing a familiar song or chorus of thanks, like the Doxology or "Thank you, Lord."

Reference Notes

BIBLE STUDY NOTES

Use these notes to gain further understanding of the text as you study on your own.

COLOSSIANS 3:12

God's chosen ones. Christians are heirs to the status of Israel as God's chosen people. But just like with Israel, the Christian is chosen not to special or exclusive privilege, but rather to a mission. Israel was to be "a light to the nations" (Isa. 49:6). Christians are chosen to spread God's message of love and redemption to all people. As we are told in 1 Peter 2:9, "But you are a chosen race, a royal priesthood, a holy nation, a people for His possession, so that you may proclaim the praises of the One who called you out of darkness into His marvelous light."

Just as the Lord has forgiven you. Throughout the New Testament, this is the most important motivator for us to forgive others. We find it implicitly in the parable of the Unforgiving Slave (Matt. 18:21-35), in the Lord's Prayer (Matt. 6:9-13), as well as in the teaching of Paul (Eph. 4:32).

the perfect bond of unity. Laws are sometimes necessary to make people relate to each other responsibly, but laws cannot truly bring us together. Only love, as it has been shown to us in Jesus Christ, can do that.

And let the peace of the Messiah ... control your hearts. "Your" is plural: What is in view is not just a sense of personal serenity, but a mutual commitment to consider peaceful relationships with one another as the highest priority in their corporate life.

the message about the Messiah. While the false teachers didn't "hold on to the Head" (2:19), the message the Colossians were to teach one another had to be centered on Jesus.

dwell richly among you. Spiritual fullness is rooted neither in secret knowledge nor in mystical experiences but in a commitment to Christ.

psalms, hymns, and spiritual songs. The psalms refer to the Old Testament Book of Psalms. Hymns were songs common to the church (Luke 1:46-55,68-79; John 1:1-18; Phil. 2:6-11; Rev. 4:8,11). Spiritual songs were spontaneous expressions of praise to Christ.

notes

notes

10

Supreme Submission

Prepare for the Session

	READINGS	REFLECTIVE QUESTIONS
Monday	Colossians 3:18-19	How difficult is it for you to submit to another person? Can you truly love, or do you get tied up in power struggles?
Tuesday	Colossians 3:20	How do you feel about the way you handled parental authority as a youth? Are you at peace with your parents now? Or are you still rebelling?
Wednesday	Colossians 3:21-22	What are you doing to encourage the children under your care or influence?
Thursday	Luke 2:41-42	What religious traditions are you passing on to your children or the children you influence?
Friday	Luke 2:51-52	What family life memories do you now treasure in your heart?
Saturday	Luke 15:11-32	Are you able to forgive other family members? If not, what holds you back?
Sunday	1 Corinthians 13:4-7	How can you live the standards of 1 Corinthians 13 in your family life today?

10

BIBLE STUDY
- to consider the roles of husband and wife and what it means to "submit" to one another
- to understand how abusive or harsh behavior can discourage a spouse or a child
- to appreciate the need for personal integrity in both private and public situations

LIFE CHANGE
- to institute the practice of a regular family meeting
- to ask one family member to share how our behavior encourages or discourages them
- to evaluate how consistent our personal integrity is in private and public situations by keeping a journal of things we do in private that we would not do in public

Icebreaker
10-15 minutes

Our Emancipation Proclamation. Go around the group on question 1 and let everyone share. Then go around again on questions 2 and 3, as time allows.

1. What is the closest you have come to feeling like a slave?

   ☐ when I was a kid and had to do what I was told
   ☐ ever since the honeymoon was over
   ☐ ever since I've had kids and had to take care of a house
   ☐ in a former job
   ☐ in my present job
   ☐ when I realized how much of my paycheck goes for taxes
   ☐ other: _____

2. What do you most feel "enslaved" by right now?

   ☐ trying to keep up with the bills   ☐ my past
   ☐ trying to maintain a house   ☐ an addiction
   ☐ being a people-pleaser—worrying about what people think
   ☐ my own workaholic tendencies
   ☐ the prejudices and stereotypes of society
   ☐ other: _____

3. Finish this sentence: "If God would issue me an 'Emancipation Proclamation' He would say ... "

Bible Study

The Scripture for this week:

LEARNING FROM THE BIBLE

COLOSSIANS 3:18–22

[18]Wives, be submissive to your husbands, as is fitting in the Lord. [19]Husbands, love your wives and don't become bitter against them.
[20]Children, obey your parents in everything, for this is pleasing in the Lord.
[21]Fathers, do not exasperate your children, so they won't become discouraged.
[22]Slaves, obey your human masters in everything; don't work only while being watched, in order to please men, but work whole-heartedly, fearing the Lord.

...about today's session

A WORD FROM THE LEADER

Write your answers here.

1. What societal problems result from the difficulty people have in walking worthy of the Lord at home?

_____

_____

_____

10

2. What person do you know who, like Atticus Finch, is a model of personal integrity?

3. Why do "false fronts" not work at home?

Identifying with the Story

In horseshoe groups of 6–8, explore questions as time allows.

1. Which of the following phrases best describes the authority structure in the home where you were raised?

   ☐ "Father knows best."
   ☐ "If Mama ain't happy, ain't nobody happy!"
   ☐ "I'm their leader—which way did they go?"
   ☐ "Dad wore the pants in the family ... when Mama let him."
   ☐ "Kids rule!"
   ☐ Mom and Dad believed in "United we stand; Divided we fall!"

2. In your immediate family, which person would you associate with each of the following words from our text for this week.

   "submissive" _____

   "bitter" _____

   "pleasing"_____

   "discouraged" _____

3. What experience did you have as a youth that made you later wish you had obeyed your parent(s)?

today's session

What is God teaching you from this story?

1. How does Jesus' teaching about servanthood put Paul's teaching about being submissive in a different light?

2. In what four situations does Scripture call us to submit to another person?

   _____

   _____

   _____

   _____

3. What attitude does being "submissive" or "subject" require, and why is this important in a family?

4. Why was the instruction for husbands not to be harsh with their wives especially important in biblical times?

5. Why is it important that a Christian's behavior be consistent at home and in public?

Learning from the Story

☖ In horseshoe groups of 6-8, choose an answer and explain why you chose what you did.

1. How does being in the Lord help you in submitting yourself to others?

2. What can you do to be a better encourager, instead of an instrument of discouragement, in your family?
   - [ ] get past my own childhood discouragements
   - [ ] learn to listen better to my family, especially to their feelings and dreams
   - [ ] look for the positive in what people are doing, instead of the negative in what they aren't doing
   - [ ] get my focus off of me
   - [ ] emulate those who have encouraged me
   - [ ] I'm doing this well already.
   - [ ] other: _____

3. What is one thing you can do to be more of a person of integrity —to be the same person in your home as you are in public?

life change lessons

1. Why is life change in a family system sometimes difficult?

2. What two things are required to change a family system?

_____

_____

Caring Time

15-20 minutes

Close by sharing prayer requests and praying for one another, especially for family members who are in need. Begin by having each group member answer the question:

"What person in your family, immediate or extended, especially needs the prayers of this group right now?"

Pray for the concerns that people share. Then move on to praying for the concerns on the Prayer/Praise Report. Continue to pray for God to guide you to someone to bring next week to fill the empty chair.

Reference Notes

Use these notes to gain further understanding of the text as you study on your own.

be submissive. In Christ, this is transformed from a passive obedience to an authority to a specific application of Christ's call to put the needs and interest of others before one's own (Eph. 5:21-24; Phil. 2:4).

**COLOSSIANS
3:19**

**COLOSSIANS
3:20**

**COLOSSIANS
3:21**

**COLOSSIANS
3:22**

love. This is the distinctively Christian *agape* love involving the willful decision to do good for another regardless of personal cost.

obey your parents. See Exodus 20:12.

Fathers. This word can mean "parents" as well (Heb. 11:23).

Slaves. Slaves were legally considered the property of their masters. While obedience was required at the threat of punishment, Paul called for an attitude of faithful service in light of the fact that, ultimately, Christ is the master of all.

10

notes

Service with a Smile

Prepare for the Session

	READINGS	REFLECTIVE QUESTIONS
Monday	Colossians 3:23	How enthusiastic are you about your faith? Have you lost the spark?
Tuesday	Colossians 3:24	How confident do you feel of the inheritance waiting for you in heaven? What could help you feel more assured by this promise?
Wednesday	Colossians 3:25–4:1	Do you sometimes envy a person with a sinful lifestyle? Are you doing all you can to witness to such people and encourage them to change?
Thursday	Nehemiah 8:5-12	Have you ever been so touched by the promises of Scripture that you were moved to tears? Are you letting Scripture truly touch your heart?
Friday	Acts 2:42-47	Are you participating in a fellowship that is full of enthusiasm and joy? What can you do to make your church more loving and joyful?
Saturday	Acts 5:41-42	Does the prospect of having to make sacrifices for Christ scare you or help you to feel "part of the team"?
Sunday	Philippians 4:4-7	Do you rejoice over what God has done or complain about what is *not* happening? How can you change that attitude?

11

BIBLE STUDY

- to consider what it means to work for the Lord with enthusiasm, and to see what can interfere with that enthusiasm
- to realize the difference between doing work to please the Lord and doing work to please people
- to be reminded of the reward we are promised in Jesus Christ, and to hold the promise of that reward before us

LIFE CHANGE

- to continue to explore any spiritual discouragements or questions we have
- to dedicate each ministry or service we are involved in to the Lord
- to post God's promises in our home

Icebreaker

10-15 minutes

**GATHERING
THE PEOPLE
◯ Form
horseshoe
groups of
6–8 people.**

Getting "Pumped." Go around the group on question 1 and let everyone share. Then go around again on questions 2 and 3, as time allows.

1. When are you most likely to get really "pumped" about something?

☐ when my favorite sports team is winning
☐ when there is a sale at my favorite store
☐ when the stock market is up
☐ when it's a beautiful day and I have time off
☐ when I get a visit from old friends
☐ when I am caught up in an exciting project
☐ when I'm at a concert by my favorite group or singer
☐ when I get to see my grandchildren
☐ when my children are honored for an achievement
☐ other: _____

2. How can other people tell when you're really enthusiastic or excited about something?

☐ I'm hyper! ☐ I'm like a kid! ☐ I say "Yippie!"
☐ I move more quickly and smile a lot!
☐ The corners of my mouth turn up ... a little.
☐ I doubt if they can tell.
☐ I'm not sure *I* can tell!

3. Finish this sentence: "The most enthusiasm I felt in church or in doing something for God was when..."

Bible Study
30-45 minutes

The Scripture for this week:

LEARNING FROM THE BIBLE

COLOSSIANS 3:23—4:1

²³Whatever you do, do it enthusiastically, as something done for the Lord and not for men, ²⁴knowing that you will receive the reward of an inheritance from the Lord—you serve the Lord Christ. ²⁵For the wrongdoer will be paid back for whatever wrong he has done, and there is no favoritism.

¹Masters, supply your slaves with what is right and fair, since you know that you too have a Master in heaven.

...about today's session

A WORD FROM THE LEADER

1. What Greek words does the word "enthusiasm" come from? What does it mean?

Write your answers here.

2. What would you say is the relationship between worship style and showing enthusiasm in your service to the Lord?

3. What reason is mentioned for why sports and entertainment fans often show more enthusiasm than Christians do for Christ? What do you think about this?

Identifying with the Story

⚲ In
horseshoe
groups of 6–8,
explore
questions as
time allows.

1. Did favoritism play a role in the family in which you were raised? How was it expressed? How did you respond?

2. In the work that you do, whether paid, volunteer, or at home, whom are you most working to please?

   ☐ A parent—I still live by their standards.
   ☐ My spouse—I want him/her to approve of what I do.
   ☐ My children—I want them to think I'm a good parent.
   ☐ My boss—I respect his/her opinion.
   ☐ Myself—I have my own high standards.
   ☐ My friends—I want to impress them with my skill and success.
   ☐ In all honesty, the Lord.
   ☐ other: _____

3. Of all the things you are called upon to do for the Lord, which one do you have the hardest time doing enthusiastically?

   ☐ studying the Bible   ☐ worshiping
   ☐ sharing my faith with others ☐ giving money
   ☐ helping people in need   ☐ other: _____
   ☐ serving on church boards or committees

today's session

1. What group did Paul primarily address in this text?

2. What four examples are given of people working in ministries to please people and not God? Can you think of others?

_____

_____

_____

_____

3. List two ways working to please people rather than God is detrimental?

_____

_____

4. What is the most important factor in determining whether a reward will make us enthusiastic for our work?

5. What rewards do we have or will we receive for working for Christ?

Learning from the Story

⋃ In horseshoe groups of 6-8, choose an answer and explain why you chose what you did.

1. What is currently limiting your enthusiasm for the Lord?

☐ the hypocrisy and political maneuvering I see in the church
☐ the distractions of the world
☐ some spiritually discouraging experiences I have had of late (like the death of a loved one)
☐ my cynicism about the Lord's promises
☐ the wrongdoers I see apparently prospering
☐ Nothing—I'm really "pumped"!
☐ other: _____

11

2. How do you feel about the wrongdoers you see in the world?

☐ Sometimes I feel a little envious of what they get away with.
☐ "Been there. Done that. Bought the t-shirt. Ready to move on."
☐ I feel sorry for them. They're heading in the wrong direction.
☐ I feel sorry for them—God will punish them.
☐ I'm kind of looking forward to God punishing them.
☐ I feel frustrated I haven't been able to do more to get through to them.
☐ other: _____

3. What most fans the flames of your enthusiasm for Christ?

☐ the other enthusiastic Christians I meet
☐ the worship services I attend
☐ my own private devotional time
☐ seeing what Christians are doing for good in the world
☐ reading the promises of God in Scripture

life change lessons

1. What are three things that can block a person's enthusiasm for a good work?

   _____

   _____

   _____

2. What is the best approach to dealing with unresolved anger at God or spiritual questions?

Caring Time

15-20 minutes

During this time, have everyone in the group share prayer requests and pray for one another. Today, let us especially pray for any spiritual wounds group members may have. Begin by having each member answer the question:

"What spiritual wound have you experienced
(a death, a disappointment, etc.)
for which you need prayer support right now?"

Pray for the wounds that people share and that God would give them healing, peace, and strength. In addition, pray for the concerns on the Prayer/Praise Report.

Reference Notes

Use these notes to gain further understanding
of the text as you study on your own.

COLOSSIANS 3:24

inheritance. The Christian looks forward to inheriting the fullness of the kingdom of God (Luke 12:32; Eph. 5:5). This hope (1:5) provides the basis for "endurance and patience" with thanksgiving (1:11-12), even in the types of hardships a slave might face.

COLOSSIANS 3:25

For the wrongdoer will be paid back for whatever wrong he has done. Whereas in Ephesians 6:8, Paul promised slaves that "the Lord will reward everyone for whatever good he does," here he warned that misbehavior will result in judgment.

there is no favoritism. Slaves, even though oppressed by their masters, cannot expect God to excuse sin (v. 22). Ephesians 6:9 applies this same phrase to masters, warning them that their position of authority will not exempt them from judgment should they abuse that authority.

COLOSSIANS 4:1

supply your slaves with what is right and fair. While Paul did not oppose slavery as such, he did call upon Christian masters to treat their slaves with justice and consideration, values which Roman law did not require of them.

you too have a Master in heaven. Masters are to relate to their slaves in the full realization that God is their Master and they are accountable to Him for their behavior toward their slaves.

11

notes

Seeker Salt

Prepare for the Session

	READINGS	REFLECTIVE QUESTIONS
Monday	Colossians 4:2	Are you able to maintain a regular, consistent prayer life? How can you be better disciplined in this area?
Tuesday	Colossians 4:3-4	When you tell friends you will pray for them, do you follow through with your promise? Why or why not?
Wednesday	Colossians 4:5	Are you reaching out to outsiders and non-Christians, or are you pulling back into the safety of familiar people who already believe?
Thursday	Colossians 4:6	Do you frequently find that you are wishing you could take back things that you said? What can you do to speak with more discipline and love?
Friday	James 5:13-16	How confident are you in the effectiveness of prayer? Do you show in your actions that you believe it can make a difference?
Saturday	James 5:19-20	What are you doing to help nonbelievers find the grace of God in Jesus Christ?
Sunday	James 3:12-13	What can you do to make your tongue more of an instrument of love and less one of destruction?

BIBLE STUDY
- to look at the importance of prayer in opening doors between nonbelievers and Jesus Christ
- to consider how we can relate to nonbelievers with wisdom
- to learn what it means for our speech to be "gracious" and to discover how to manifest such speech to nonbelievers

LIFE CHANGE
- to develop and maintain a prayer list of people who need to open their heart to Jesus
- to meet someone who is not a Christian and learn three interesting facts about that person
- to have a trusted friend help us evaluate how we speak to strangers

Icebreaker
10-15 minutes

Open Doors. Go around the group on question 1 and let everyone share. Then go around again on questions 2 and 3, as time allows.

**GATHERING
THE PEOPLE
Form
horseshoe
groups of
6–8 people.**

1. To which of the following would you most like to have an "open door" anytime you wished to enter?

☐ Madison Square Garden ☐ the Oval Office
☐ The Smithsonian Institute ☐ Disney World
☐ the locker room of my favorite sports team
☐ the floor of the New York Stock Exchange
☐ my favorite celebrity's wardrobe
☐ the conference room of a business rival
☐ other: _____

2. In which of the following situations in your life do you feel you have an open door (no big barriers and/or lots of opportunity)? In which of them do you feel the "door" is closed (communication is shut down, opportunities are few)? Write by each one either "O" for open or "C" for closed.

____ your marriage or most intimate relationship
____ your profession
____ your relationship with your children
____ your relationship to God
____ your future in general

3. Finish this sentence: "The door I would like to see open for our class or group would be the door to ..."

Bible Study

30-45 minutes

The Scripture for this week:

LEARNING
FROM THE
BIBLE

COLOSSIANS
4:2–6

²*Devote yourselves to prayer; stay alert in it with thanksgiving.* ³*At the same time, pray also for us that God may open a door to us for the message, to speak the mystery of the Messiah—for which I am in prison—* ⁴*so that I may reveal it as I am required to speak.* ⁵*Walk in wisdom toward outsiders, making the most of the time.* ⁶*Your speech should always be gracious, seasoned with salt, so that you may know how you should answer each person.*

...about today's session

**A WORD
FROM THE
LEADER**

**Write your
answers
here.**

1. What are two drawbacks of the Internet in relation to opening doors to others?

_____

_____

2. What two groups closed doors to Paul in his time?

_____

_____

3. What were three actions Paul suggested to the Colossians for helping to open doors for Christ?

_____

_____

_____

12

Identifying with the Story

In horseshoe groups of 6–8, explore questions as time allows.

1. In the course of your lifetime, whom have you most often seen as "outsiders"?

☐ people from other parts of the country ("Yankees," New Yorkers, Californians, etc.)
☐ agitators for a minority political cause
☐ people of other races   ☐ foreigners
☐ farmers and country people   ☐ homeless people
☐ people with addictions   ☐ non-Christians
☐ me   ☐ other: _____

2. What would you say is the biggest or most noticeable barrier between you and the outsider group you mentioned in question 1 (or between you and others if your response was "me")?

☐ the demands they make on me and my culture
☐ the way they talk   ☐ the way they dress
☐ just different life experiences ☐ the way they think
☐ different values and beliefs   ☐ other: _____

3. What have you found to be most effective in opening doors with the outsider group you mentioned in question 1?

☐ plain old talking and listening
☐ finding shared interests—a common value or cause
☐ finding shared interests—like in sports, the arts, or music
☐ praying and worshiping with them
☐ taking the risk of reaching out
☐ working on projects where we have a common interest
☐ I have never tried
☐ other: _____

today's session

What is God teaching you from this story?

1. How was Paul's view on "outsiders" different than that of the traditional Jew of the time?

2. In Paul's day why didn't Christians think of themselves as "outsiders," even though they had reason to?

3. What four positive results had the church already experienced from the power of prayer before Paul wrote these words?

_____

_____

_____

_____

4. List three possible, but somewhat deficient, ways of relating to outsiders.

_____

_____

_____

5. What did Paul mean by having speech "seasoned with salt" (v. 6)?

Learning from the Story

In horseshoe groups of 6-8, choose an answer and explain why you chose what you did.

1. What is God calling you to do to better reach out to those outside the faith?

- [ ] to stop being so protective of myself and to take risks
- [ ] to keep this need in my prayers
- [ ] to listen to nonbelievers more
- [ ] to have more courage in saying what I believe
- [ ] to learn to speak more positively
- [ ] to move out of my small circle of friends
- [ ] other: _____

12

2. Which of the following do you think is most important for speech to be gracious?

☐ having a gentle tone
☐ avoiding negative or judgmental statements
☐ referring often to Christ and God's love
☐ affirming the person with whom you are talking
☐ being honest and sincere
☐ avoiding sarcasm and inflammatory statements

3. How would you say you are doing in the area of showing "gracious" speech?

☐ Great—my words are as sweet as honey.
☐ Well, SOME of them are as honey ... overall, more like sweet and sour sauce.
☐ My speech can be gracious when I set my mind to it.
☐ My speech has some pretty rough edges.
☐ I tell it like it is ... and sometimes that's not very pretty!
☐ other: _____

life change lessons

How can you apply this session to your life?

Write your answers here.

1. When a person closes the door of his or her heart to Jesus, why doesn't Christ just "knock the door down" and force His way in?

2. In the book of Revelation, before what church did Jesus promise to set "an open door" (Rev. 3:8)? What does that say to the modern church?

Caring Time

15-20 minutes

CARING TIME

♡ **Remain in horseshoe groups of 6-8.**

Come together now for a time of sharing and prayer. Begin by listening to each other's dreams for the class or group by having each group member answer the following question:

"What doors would you like to see open for this group as we head on to other studies and think of new challenges?"

Pray for the dreams that people share. Then move on to praying for the concerns on the Prayer/Praise Report.

Reference Notes

Use these notes to gain further understanding
of the text as you study on your own.

BIBLE STUDY NOTES

COLOSSIANS 4:2

Devote yourselves to prayer. See the example of the church in Acts 1:14; 2:42; and 6:4.
stay alert. An allusion to Matthew 26:41 and Luke 18:1. This call to vigilance and spiritual alertness became part of the apostles' teaching to Christians in general (Acts 20:31; 1 Cor. 16:13; 1 Thess. 5:6; 1 Pet. 5:8).

COLOSSIANS 4:3

the mystery of the Messiah. See 1:25-27.
in prison. Paul, imprisoned several times because Jewish opponents considered his missionary activity as subversive to their interests, probably wrote this letter while under the house arrest described in Acts 28.

COLOSSIANS 4:4

that I may reveal it as I am required to speak. In Ephesians 6:20, Paul asked for prayer that he might speak fearlessly. He knew that soon his case would come before the emperor.

COLOSSIANS 4:5

outsiders. By this Paul meant nonbelieving neighbors and associates.
making the most of the time. A similar passage in Ephesians 5:15 refers to the Christian's general conduct. In view here, however, is the special importance of being alert to God-given opportunities to bear witness to Christ in the course of daily life.

COLOSSIANS 4:6

seasoned with salt. Since salt was used to preserve food and prevent corruption, this metaphor has the same import as Paul's words in Ephesians 4:29. The Christian's witness is not to be argumentative or arrogant, but respectful and gracious (2 Tim. 2:23-26).

12

notes

13

Teamtastic!

Prepare for the Session

	READINGS	REFLECTIVE QUESTIONS
Monday	Colossians 4:7-11	Who has encouraged your heart recently? Have you thanked that person for what they have done?
Tuesday	Colossians 4:12-15	For whom, besides yourself and your immediate family, are you working hard? Are you helping others to "stand mature" in the Lord (v. 12)?
Wednesday	Colossians 4:16-18	Is there a ministry Christ has given you to which you need to pay more attention?
Thursday	John 15:12-15	When have you developed friendships while working with others for Christ? What do you need to do to strengthen these friendships?
Friday	Luke 22:28-30	When your friends go through hard times, are you there for them? How are you showing support to them?
Saturday	Philippians 1:3-6	What have you begun that you need to make sure to finish? What support will you need from others to do this?
Sunday	Acts 20:32-38	When have you had to say good-bye to Christian friends? What memories of them and your experiences together remain in your heart?

13

BIBLE STUDY
- to see what made the Christians who worked with Paul such an effective ministry team
- to consider ways to encourage one another in the faith
- to acknowledge the importance focusing on ministry goals has for effective team ministry

LIFE CHANGE
- to choose one leader in our church to encourage in some way each week
- to commit to praying daily for our pastor or pastoral team
- to obtain our church's mission statement and find one thing we can do to help make that mission happen

Icebreaker

10-15 minutes

GATHERING
THE PEOPLE
〇 Form
horseshoe
groups of
6–8 people.

A Great Team! Go around the group on question 1 and let everyone share. Then go around again on questions 2 and 3, as time allows.

1. Looking back over your life, what is the greatest "team" experience that you've had?

   ☐ a sports team in junior high or high school
   ☐ a drama cast I was in during high school
   ☐ a sports team I was on in college or as an adult
   ☐ a drama cast I was in during college or as an adult
   ☐ a project team at work
   ☐ a ministry or mission team
   ☐ a team that worked on a community project
   ☐ other: _____

2. What do you enjoy the most about being part of a great team?

   ☐ WINNING!
   ☐ the camaraderie
   ☐ all the attention I get from the crowd
   ☐ doing something that makes a difference
   ☐ feeling I can contribute and that I am needed

☐ the satisfaction that comes from accomplishment
☐ getting to know people better
☐ other: _____

3. If you could assemble a team to work on one problem or area of need right now, what problem or need would you choose?

Bible Study

30-45 minutes

The Scripture for this week:

LEARNING FROM THE BIBLE

COLOSSIANS 4:7–18

[7]*Tychicus, a loved brother, a faithful servant, and a fellow slave in the Lord, will tell you all the news about me.* [8]*I have sent him to you for this very purpose, so that you may know how we are, and so that he may encourage your hearts.* [9]*He is with Onesimus, a faithful and loved brother, who is one of you. They will tell you about everything here.*

[10]*Aristarchus, my fellow prisoner, greets you, as does Mark, Barnabas' cousin (concerning whom you have received instructions: if he comes to you, welcome him),* [11]*and so does Jesus who is called Justus. These alone of the circumcision are my co-workers for the kingdom of God, and they have been a comfort to me.* [12]*Epaphras, who is one of you, a slave of Christ Jesus, greets you. He is always contending for you in his prayers, so that you can stand mature and fully assured in everything God wills.* [13]*For I testify about him that he works hard for you, for those in Laodicea, and for those in Hierapolis.* [14]*Luke, the loved physician, and Demas greet you.* [15]*Give my greetings to the brothers in Laodicea, and to Nympha and the church in her house.* [16]*And when this letter has been read among you, have it read also in the church of the Laodiceans; and see that you also read the letter from Laodicea.* [17]*And tell Archippus, "Pay attention to the ministry you have received in the Lord, so that you can accomplish it."*

[18]*This greeting is in my own hand—Paul. Remember my imprisonment. Grace be with you.*

13

...about today's session

A WORD FROM THE LEADER

Write your answers here.

1. How do you see the emphasis in our country on individualism affecting the work of the church?

2. What are two reasons why a "star" approach to ministry most often does not work?

   _____

   _____

3. What are some factors that make ministering in today's world complicated?

Identifying with the Story

⟲ In horseshoe groups of 6–8, explore questions as time allows.

1. What friends do you have who fill the same functions as the following people did for Paul or for the Christians at Colossae?

   · Tychicus—the communicator, the one who keeps you informed about old friends away from you _____

   · Aristarchus—the "fellow prisoner," the one who has been through a lot with you _____

   · Onesimus & Epaphras—the "kindred spirits," the ones who are closest to you _____ & _____

   · Epaphras—the prayer warrior, the one who has "always contended for you" in his or her prayers _____

   · Mark & Justus—the comforters, the ones who have done the most to lift you when you were down _____ & _____

2. What would you tell someone who hasn't seen you for a while about your life that might encourage their heart?

3. What difficulty in your life would you like people to remember right now, as Paul wanted people to remember his imprisonment?

today's session

1. What are four factors that made the team Paul assembled a great ministerial team?

_____

_____

_____

_____

2. Who were some people Paul sent to the churches to encourage them?

_____

_____

_____

3. Why was mutual encouragement so important in Paul's time?

4. What are some examples of the "hard work" that people like Epaphras had to do as part of Paul's team?

_____

_____

_____

_____

13

5. What did Paul see as his own life goal, as reported in Philippians?

Learning from the Story

⟲ In horseshoe groups of 6-8, choose an answer and explain why you chose what you did.

1. What would you say is the best way for Christians to "encourage each other's hearts"?

   ⬭ affirming the good things that I see them doing
   ⬭ telling what I have seen God doing in my life
   ⬭ listening to them
   ⬭ reminding them of the promises of God
   ⬭ other: _____

2. What needs to happen for members of this group to more effectively "contend for each other in prayer"?

3. What is the main thing that diverts your attention from focusing on your ministry? When this happens, what can members of this class do to help you regain your focus?

life change lessons

How can you apply this session to your life?

Write your answers here.

1. In order to build a "winning team," what two things must we do?

   _____

   _____

2. In what four ways can we encourage one another?

_____

_____

_____

_____

Caring Time
15-20 minutes

CARING TIME

Pray for the concerns listed on the Prayer/Praise Report, then continue with the evaluation and covenant.

Remain in horseshoe groups of 6-8.

1. Take some time to evaluate the life of your group by using the statements below. Read the first sentence out loud and ask everyone to explain where they would put a dot between the two extremes. When you are finished, go back and give your group an overall grade in the categories of Group Building, Bible Study, and Mission.

GROUP BUILDING

On celebrating life and having fun together, we were more like a ...
wet blanket · hot tub

On becoming a caring community, we were more like a ...
prickly porcupine · cuddly teddy bear

 BIBLE STUDY

On sharing our spiritual stories, we were more like a ...
shallow pond · spring-fed lake

On digging into Scripture, we were more like a ...
slow-moving snail · voracious anteater

 MISSION

On inviting new people into our group, we were more like a ...
barbed-wire fence ···················· wide-open door

On stretching our vision for mission, we were more like an ...
ostrich ································· eagle

2. What are some specific areas in which you have grown in this course?

☐ being more open to the Holy Spirit's guidance
☐ finding new ways to minister to other's needs
☐ handling conflict situations in the church with love and wisdom
☐ sharing faith and fellowship with other cultures
☐ understanding the power of prayer
☐ slowing down and letting the Holy Spirit guide me
☐ following ethical business practices
☐ other:_____

A covenant is a promise made to another in the presence of God. Its purpose is to indicate your intention to make yourselves available to one another for the fulfillment of the purposes you share in common. If your group is going to continue, in a spirit of prayer work your way through the following sentences, trying to reach an agreement on each statement pertaining to your ongoing life together. Write out your covenant like a contract, stating your purpose, goals, and the ground rules for your group.

1. The purpose of our group will be:

2. Our goals will be:

3. We will meet on _____ (day of week).

4. We will meet for _____ weeks, after which we will decide if we wish to continue as a group.

5. We will meet from _____ to _____ and we will strive to start on time and end on time.

6. We will meet at _____ (place) or we will rotate from house to house.

7. We will agree to the following ground rules for our group (check):

☐ PRIORITY: While you are in this course of study, you give the group meetings priority.

☐ PARTICIPATION: Everyone is encouraged to participate and no one dominates.

☐ RESPECT: Everyone has the right to his or her own opinion, and all questions are encouraged and respected.

☐ CONFIDENTIALITY: Anything said in the meeting is never repeated outside the meeting.

☐ LIFE CHANGE: We will regularly assess our own life change goals and encourage one another in our pursuit of Christlikeness.

☐ EMPTY CHAIR: The group stays open to reaching new people at every meeting.

☐ CARE and SUPPORT: Permission is given to call upon each other at any time especially in times of crisis. The group will provide care for every member.

☐ ACCOUNTABILITY: We agree to let the members of the group hold us accountable to the commitments which each of us make in whatever loving ways we decide upon.

☐ MISSION: We will do everything in our power to start a new group.

☐ MINISTRY: The group will encourage one another to volunteer and serve in a ministry, and to support missions by giving financially and/or personally serving.

13

Reference Notes

Use these notes to gain further understanding
of the text as you study on your own.

**COLOSSIANS
4:7**

Tychicus. Tychicus was a traveling companion of Paul in Acts 20:4.

**COLOSSIANS
4:9**

Onesimus. The converted slave was the subject of the letter to Philemon.
one of you. A fellow Colossian.

**COLOSSIANS
4:10**

Aristarchus. Another person mentioned in Acts 20:4 as traveling with Paul.
Mark, Barnabas' cousin. Barnabas and Paul had had a "parting of the
ways" over whether Mark should be included on their second missionary
journey after he had deserted them on the first journey (Acts 13:13; 15:36-
41). This passage shows that there was a rapprochement between Mark
and Paul. Paul lists him as one of his few Jewish co-workers and as one
who had been a "comfort" to him.

**COLOSSIANS
4:11**

Jesus who is called Justus. Jesus was a rather common name of the time.
Nothing is really known of this person other than what is written here.

**COLOSSIANS
4:12**

Epaphras. A native Colossian who established the church there and
throughout the Lycus valley (1:7; Philem. 23). Paul's commendation here
and in 1:7 substantiates his claim that the church had already heard the
whole gospel.
a slave of Christ Jesus. Paul used this phrase elsewhere to describe himself (Rom. 1:1; Phil. 1:1). In so doing he both identified with and exalted
the low estate of actual slaves in his call to them to render service as to
the Lord (3:24). This further commendation of Epaphras would help
assure the Colossians that he had indeed passed along the gospel to them.
always contending for you in his prayers. One dimension of devotion
to prayer (4:2) is the realization that it is an encounter not only with God
but against spiritual forces that seek to hinder God's work (Eph. 6:12).
This was especially needed as the Colossians faced the challenge of the
false teachers.
fully assured. Another "fullness" word to encourage the Colossian believers that in Christ they had all God has to bestow on people.

**COLOSSIANS
4:13**

Laodicea. A city just a few miles from Colossae, near the Lycus River.
Hierapolis. A city about twelve miles northwest of Colossae and six miles
north of Laodicea.

**COLOSSIANS
4:14**

Luke, the loved physician. This reference reveals Luke's profession. The
various "we" passages in the book of Acts (16:10-17; 20:5–21:18;
27:1–28:16) indicate that Luke accompanied Paul at several points in his
missionary work.

Nympha and the church in her house. The Laodicean church, or at least part of it, followed the custom of other early churches in meeting in the homes of members who could accommodate them. Philemon's home was the site of the congregation in Colossae (Philem. 1-2).

The epistles were written to address specific problems and concerns of the various churches to which they were written. They were meant to be read at gatherings of the church.

the letter from Laodicea. Some have thought that this might be what is now our letter to the Ephesians since no specific destination is mentioned in that letter. It is more likely that this is a lost letter, like the one Paul refers to in 2 Corinthians 2:4,9.

Archippus. Philemon 2 calls him a "fellow soldier." Since he is the only Colossian specifically addressed in the letter, he may have been a leading elder in the church.

This greeting is in my own hand—Paul. Typically, others actually wrote Paul's letters at his dictation (Rom. 16:22) while he penned the final greeting as a mark of the letter's genuineness (1 Cor. 16:21; Gal. 6:11; 2 Thess. 3:17; Philem. 19). Second Thessalonians 2:2 hints at the possibility that forged letters had been circulated in Paul's name.

Grace be with you. Paul's common greeting sums up the essence of his message to this church—that they are saved completely through the gracious work of Jesus Christ on their behalf.

13

notes

notes

notes

notes

notes

notes

notes

notes

notes

**PASS THIS DIRECTORY AROUND AND
HAVE YOUR GROUP MEMBERS FILL IN
THEIR NAMES AND PHONE NUMBERS.**

Group
Directory

NAME   **PHONE**